I believe all writers ha
in the beginning, it is t

KINDRED

In Her Eyes/ In Her Mind

By
Hellen Nakhone Madadi and
Rose Terranova Cirigliano

Edited by Rose Terranova Cirigliano

Published by

ROSE BOOKS

In affiliation with Ave U Publisher
(since 2015)

QUEENS   BROOKLYN   LONDON
ROME   SAN FRANCISCO

Introductions
By Hellen Nakhone Madadi

It's been said the world over that necessity is the mother of invention. During the first Covid 19 wave, unemployed, I discovered that I needed to fill the void. I took it upon myself to dig deep into the life of one amazing lady, Malaika. Her inner child was haunted and in turmoil. The adult later becomes a product of past pains unresolved.

***

By Rose Terranova Cirigliano

Each one of us has a personal history, which has interacted with the "self" we inherited from our parents that has played a part in molding us into the "person" we have become. Although our cultures differ, along with the society, environment and geography, in the end our basic humanity comes through. The basic survival instinct is immutable.

At the center of our being there is something powerful and apart from our ego. It searches for meaning and purpose until it finds expression and fulfills a destiny, of which we are most often unaware. Socrates said, "An unexamined life is not worth living."

Here are two examined lives.

IN HER EYES

By

Hellen Nakhone Madadi

IN HER MIND

By

Rose Terranova Cirigliano

8

Malaika

"I remember looking at her eyes and all I could see was frustration, anger, and just plain disgust. The tone of her voice almost put a rubber stamp to what her eyes could not say. This woman just didn't like what she saw every time she got close to me" , said Malaika.

"But why? ", I asked Malaika shockingly at such a revelation.

Yes, that's my mother, a woman who had carried me in her womb for seven months until her belly got fed up with the weight.

"Yes, to me it appeared like I had been a weight to her for many years. That she could seize any opportunity to get me out of her sight", went on Malaika, with a far off look in her eyes.

"Malaika, are you sure you are ready to have this conversation today? I mean, we have been friends for many years. I am not going anywhere. It can wait."

"No! I'm ready to heal the wounds of many years of despair, turmoil and anguish."

Mama Malaika. That's what they called her in the village. She was schooled like many others of her time by the missionaries. Got married to one of the same who had attended missionaries schools. They travelled together and got children together. Life seemed perfect, just too perfect, they say, to be true.

The boys were boys, and girls were girls. Just that for Malaika it was extraordinary.

She had even got used to surprises. After years of great "shock absorbers" unpleasant events, she put on a shield to ward off the pain.

***

Little Frank was only two months old when Irene found she was pregnant again. "Irish Twins" was the slang term for it. Irene was 34 when she married Frank, and she wanted children, but this was a bit faster than she expected.

She met Frank at "Night Slipper" where they both worked making shoes. He was a widower with two children, and he had a kind smile and good sense of humor. Irene had pretty much given up on finding a husband. The war had recently ended. And in the 1940s you were an old maid by the time you reached 25 without any prospects.

Irene was an excellent worker. She had a sharp mind, good people skills, and climbed the "ladder" at work at a very young age becoming a supervisor of people ten years her senior. But she had pluck, and was well liked by her bosses and co-workers.

One Friday after cashing his paycheck, Frank had put his wallet on the shelf above his work station. When it was time to go home he discovered his money had been stolen. His co-workers took up a collection and replaced his lost money. Three weeks later it happened again, and one of the other workers made a disparaging remark. Irene found herself getting hot under the collar about it. That was when she realized she was in love with him.

Weeks later while he was escorting her home on the train he asked her what she would require in the man she would want to marry. She said, "A sense of humor, a sense of decency and common sense. And in that order." So he asked her if she thought he could fill the bill. And she said "Yes." And so they became engaged.

Of course he made arrangements to meet her father and ask for her hand in marriage. It was the only time Irene ever saw him wear a hat. It was a wonderful fedora, but with his Italian good looks she thought it made him look like a gangster to her father. He removed that hat and never wore another one.

Frank had two children. John and Rose, named for his father and mother, in Sicilian fashion. Rose was also his first wife's name. She was a few years older than Frank, but when he met her he was struck by the Sicilian Thunderbolt.

Rose was the forelady in a dress factory. It was during the depression and jobs were scarce. Frank had recently lost his business; the one his father had given him for a wedding present but then had to take back when the market crashed. His father needed the business to take care of Frank's ten siblings.

Rose worked hard and made a decent salary. One day a neighbor asked her if she could get a job for her son who was desperately in need of a job. Unfortunately, the job went to someone else and this neighbor held Rose responsible. She was so angry that she cursed Rose. She sent her a little doll in a box that would bear the curse; that she should not live to see her children, or her children's children grow.

Weeks later Rose read her death in her tea leaves and had a breakdown. She insisted she was dying, and Frank called the family doctor who told him he could do nothing for her. That Frank should just take her to the hospital. He no longer knew what to do. And so Frank rushed with her to the hospital. She expired in the hallway while Frank was filling out forms for her admission.

He was in shock. In the coroner's report it said that Rose had had a car accident a few weeks prior and complained that maybe this was an aftereffect. They ruled Frank out as a possible suspect in her death, even though there was no reason for her to have died. She'd simply expired; scared herself to death.

By himself Frank could not care for John and little Rose who were 5 and 3 years of age, respectively. John stayed with Frank's family. His sister Maria was there as was his youngest sibling, Tony. Tony was John's uncle, though two months younger than him, Frank's mother being pregnant at the same time as Rose.

Little Rose stayed with Rose's mother, who held her close as she grieved the loss of her eldest. She resented Irene, because with Irene's arrival on the scene, Frank would take back Rose.

Frank truly believed that Irene was sent so that he could have his family back together. Irene's idealism made her eager to be the new parent. She did not realize that she had enemies. Did not realize she was judged constantly by Rose's maternal Grandmother, who little Rose visited every Sunday along with her brother, John. They spent Sunday mornings with Rose's mom, and the afternoon with Irene's family.

And Rose's mother would grill them trying to find out if Irene was abusing them in some way. Eventually John told them to stop, and defended Irene because he could see how much their opinions and criticisms hurt her, and he could see that she meant well.

***

This is where it all began

Almost thirty something years back.

One night Malaika was sleeping in her bed and she had very scary dreams.

Tossing and turning. Sweating, gripping the sheets and squeezing crying in her dreams to run from this black monster in her sleep. She would wake up from her delirious state crying only to find herself alone and no one to hug or tell her it was just but a dream.

On good days she would sleep dreamless only for this hope to be shattered in the morning by her mother almost zapping her out of her sleep with angry shouts

Mama Malaika wasn't impressed by her daughter's drowsy state. She wanted her daughter perfect at all times. The poor young soul didn't understand her shrewd mother - perfection her middle name - always beating her for being slow.

In fear, Malaika got to make many mistakes because she always heard her mother's angry voice in her head, "Hurry up! Do it quickly!"

One time Malaika got ill, which was almost part of her; having been born premature she had a very low immunity.

She used to cry herself even more sick because she hated being in this state. It only made her mother very angry.

On this specific day Malaika had malaria. One of those tropical diseases that attacked many under age children. The medication given at that time was the best that was given for such a prognosis. The dosage was a three day oral intervention.

Unfortunately, many who took it ended up with retching bowels from every opening of the body on day two.

Malaika was in so much pain. Every muscle ached. Her head throbbed. Her nose was wet and running.

Malaika called out mother crying out from the toilet. Clenching her tiny body and tummy.

Mother who was passing by the corridor. Told her angrily " make sure you don't mess the floor and if you do clean it up quickly."

Malaika had never felt so embarrassed.

I think in her head she had pictured mother holding her calmly.

On such days when she got so sick she only remembered her father mopping her, giving her medicine and even helping feed her with a bowl of soup that mother had made.

Malaika was a fighter. She always came through like a warrior in the battlefield.

A story is told of this girl having survived death at birth.

Somewhere around the time she was in the incubator, a tremendous earth tremor took place. People were injured in that hospital. Others died outside the village but alas! This girl survived.

Her mother and father were losing their minds gravely worrying about what would become of their little lifeless baby struggling to grow in a glass vacuum.

Rushing, sweating and shaken; expecting the worst, they arrived only to find her alive and well.

After the whole incident was over, everyone was given a go ahead to leave. The young parents stayed on behind until the nurses chased them away with reassurance that things would be well and that baby would be able to go home soon.

The parents left her behind.

Friends, as you read this you should realise that Malaika had been taught to be independent from before she was even born.

***

Years ago when I was in training to be a rap group facilitator we did this exercise. We were given a drawing of a swimming pool. On one side was a diving board. On the second side there was a slide, and on the third side there was a ladder. The activity was that if the pool represented major events or transition points in your life, how did you enter the pool. Did you dive right in and take control, or did you slide in willy nilly and land wherever you landed and enjoy the adventure. Or did you enter cautiously by slowly entering the water going down the ladder gradually. When it came to be my turn to say how I entered the pool, I shrugged my shoulders and said, "Somebody pushed me."

And that has been a pattern of my life. Unexpected, not foreseen, and unintentionally I am thrown into my life's major events or turning points.

There is not a plan that I ever made that came to be. Every plan was derailed by an unexpected life altering occurrence. Believe me, I did not plan things that way.... Lol.

Many of these events resulted in a level of trauma, sometimes disassociative, and other times just overwhelmingly sad and depressing, which made me do a tremendous amount of walking through the streets crying.

When I was eleven I almost drowned in a lake. I left my body and remember watching myself from above and behind myself. And not talking. My father's death when I was 16 took me another 25 years to process.

My next emotional breakdown happened when I was 20, and my oldest brother was dying, and died of pancreatic cancer, my other brother was shooting heroin, and my third brother was out hotwiring cars. I kind of disappeared ... lots of walking and crying.

Anger brought me back. Anger at betrayal by someone I had turned to for help. ... in the end I have this pattern.... And I do not think I created it. It's just the way things go.... Nothing is in my control. Never was, never will be.

Any of the traumas that I survived with some grace were ones when I actually had someone who loved me, cared about me, and helped me. There are certain things in life you need help for. That's where man got that genetic instinct to seek the safety of community. Better for survival. So it is a part of survival instinct. Seeking to belong somewhere. Seeking support and community.

The only thing I ever remember being applauded for was caring for and interacting with children. I was a natural born caregiver and nurturer. So my career choices moved me in that direction.

I felt fulfilled. I felt I was a contributing member of society. I was respected. And then I was demolished. Lost everything.

It doesn't matter in the end how many times this cycle has spiralled through my life; at what ages; 11, 16, 20, 27, 33, 40, 50, 60... I am now approaching 70. And my life is being swept away.

I can not do this without help. And the only help available is the grace of God.

But trauma.... Oh well.... Stroke? Heart attack? Hysterical numbness?

I have survived cancer, twice now. And I have survived heartbreak and the death of a loved one. I have survived for 10 years now through my latest nightmare, but

All bets are off
I fly with no idea where to touch down
There is no longer ground
There is no longer a place I can go
where they have to take me in...

I am lost
I am lost
I am lost

I will survive
Beats the hell out of me how
But maybe
Just maybe
Someone will provide
A beneficial shove.

***

"Mother loves me, mother loves me, mother loves me!!" I said those words to myself as if I was possessed with anguish, fear and loneliness. I had even learnt to talk to myself. I would tell myself, "Malaika, don't cry. Even if she hits you, don't cry, you will be fine!!"

That was after a beating or two. Sometimes, she was mad with anger at something her daughter had not done as per instructions.

Malaika was one bold, very English- speaking, outspoken little girl among her friends who came for play dates. As she grew she became more cautious of her words and her environment as she began to understand the meaning of words everyday.

Her body had swellings here or there. Scar tissue here or there. Her soft skin didn't show much as it healed and left skin as new.

The six year old girl asked her mother for money to buy a samosa at school. Everyone was buying something from school using the money their parents had given them. Mother rejected her request.

The next day at school she could not wait for break time to buy the much talked about samosa.

She bought and broke it into pieces to share with friends.

That evening was one of the worst.

Mother had been waiting for her daughter to arrive from school, to unleash some thorough beating. Screaming and wailing as mother lit a match stick and held her daughter's knuckles pressed down her palms to burn her hands.

Mother said, repeat after me!! "I will not steal again."

She was 7.

They were just burns, not much although it scalded. It was very painful. She tried to eat with one hand, and bathe with one hand. The mere fact that mother had done it was enough to put Malaika in her place.

Docile and timid; all common sense left her brain that day. She became worse in school. If she was scoring low, she even went much lower. Every time mother threatened her she actually believed it. Once she had said she would tie her on the electric poles. It was just a threat but Malaika believed everything she said. You see women in the village were known at that time for using the rod to their best knowledge. They repeated, in local language.

"Spare the rod and spoil the child." Mother in this regard didn't want her daughter spoiled.

Days when schools closed, Malaika knew she had become the lowest in grades because most times that the teachers would be teaching, she was passed out from less sleep the night before. Since her brain was always worried about failing to wake up early and make her breakfast and get a reprimand or beating. She woke up very exhausted from having not slept.

This girl turned 9. Once her mother beat her so badly that she got bold and ran away.

The only place she thought she would be safe was at her former teacher's home, some distance away. She reached it bare footed with split bleeding feet as she had dashed out screaming with no time for shoes. In her little head Malaika begged her former teacher to let her stay with her.

The teacher calmed her down and as her crying ceased, Malaika was returned back home. It was believed that it took a village to raise a child so you can imagine what her former teacher said and how the rest of the evening went.

Mrs William, her former teacher, asked her mother to forgive her.

Mother was furious.

Yes, it seemed her life was full of lashes to a point where Malaika' heart became stone cold. She would feel the pain but she blocked the harsh words and cared less.

One night in anguish and solemn. Malaika decided she would take her life. She was tired of living. Her life felt worthless. The woman she wanted so much to please was never pleased. Her mother found her slow, weak, and unintelligent, unlike the other children.

Her father on the other hand was too busy at work to notice. Malaika did a great job at hiding and becoming invisible in everyone's presence.

As Malaika had heard of stories in school that when you swallow the battery of a watch you would die, she got one of those disco watches.

Took out its battery. She had water in a glass as she sat on the cold floor ready to take her own life.

She was strong-willed. She had even imagined how they would find her.

That night in the darkness of oblivion as her hand slowly approached her lips with hot tears in her eyes. Malaika heard a voice loud and clear, very defined but calm.

Malaika shook as she heard the voice of God call her name in that dark cold room. "Malaika, don't do it, my child !"

In that instant the battery fell out of her hand, she shook and wept, crashed but silently. Her whole body trembled. That night she cried herself to sleep and woke up in delirium as she had cried herself into a fever. No one knew her ordeal as she had become great at a disguise.

She was so young and at the age of nine she knew that God existed and she was never alone.

She even started praying.

***

Thinking about death, and in particular, people who mourn a loss forever.

The first person I knew who died was my mother's father. I was 4 years old. I remember him sitting in his rocking chair smoking his pipe. And I remember my mom being very sad.

The next death was of my father's father. I was 11 years old, and he had lived with us. He spoke only Italian. I remember he smoked De Nobili cigars, and ate a raw egg every morning with his cup of black coffee. We'd play two handed pinochle. He had diabetes and had his toe removed. When he went back into the hospital he told my dad to call all his children to come and say good-bye. All 8 of my father's siblings and their families arrived... What a party! And then he passed, and they all came back. There was joy in memories and much love in the house. I experienced my first wake.

The next death was 5 years later when I was 16; my dad died. It took me 30 years to accept it. The next death was my brother, Charlie. I was 20. We watched him die over the course of 9 months from pancreatic cancer. He was 85 pounds when they laid him in the coffin. I had an emotional breakdown. My first breakdown.

Four years later my sister's husband died the same way when she was in her 9th month of pregnancy. I was 25. I hated God.

Three years later, my friend and mentor, who was the same age as my brother, Charlie, died of cancer. I relived all the prior deaths again.

Ten years passed and then my sister was diagnosed with terminal cancer. Her death was catastrophic to my life. I was 40 and had my second nervous breakdown.

Shortly before her death my youngest brother was diagnosed with AIDs, and my mom had her 5th stroke. My mom passed when I was 42.

At 50 I lost my aunt, my mom's sister who was a second mother to me, and later that same year, my lover of 10 years. I removed myself from the world as best I could. Buried myself in work. And grieved all the death all over again.

I mourned Bill, and missed him. But I had been abandoned before, so I had learned to accept the desertion. And to not hold onto pointless longing. I learned to feed my soul, nurture my spirit, immerse myself in creativity... my imagination was always my most effective survival mechanism.... Or really, at this stage, my technique.

I always say, I travel with an entourage of souls..... Mourn???? What is that? Miss them??? Too many to miss every day. Too many to live longing and wishing they were back. Too many years have gone by and too many other things have happened. My own cancer dance for one. I am numb to death...

There is just my life now and the people in it. And I think about my own death every day. I have had a full life. Filled with much much more than grief. You must embrace life and not death. Celebrate the lives that we knew, and dance with others. Life is too short, and they have gone on. Let them rest in peace. Give yourself some peace.

***

Almost into her teen years. She had sought solace in her friend's home. She would pass by for tea and bread every morning and evening. Their mother seemed nicer and she was never angry.

They had a cat. Since most times she would miss breakfast as punishment for waking up late. She was eager and hungry for what her friend's home offered.

Her friend had an older brother. He would tell jokes to the girls and make them laugh. He went away to study abroad. He got back as Malaika had become a teen.

She thought he was the coolest big brother she never had.

She always looked forward to him passing by school to bring them all some chips. On their birthdays he would even surprise them with gifts of candy. They were three in the same school; his younger twin sisters and Malaika.

As fate would have it years into her highschool life, although they had kept in touch through letter writing, she discovered she had her first boy crush.

During holidays she would wish their paths crossed. They had been separated by distance. She would pray about it.

***

The crocuses are sprouting

from the cold wintry earth

Telling us Spring is coming

once again, despite the dirth

The forsythia will appear next

Yellow tips on stems sprinkle sunlight

Underscoring the cycle of life

everything returns again making things all
right

***

Although her life with mother never got any better. Malaika had now discovered avenues to channel her pain. She learned to read. Books would enable her to travel across oceans. She even went over the hills and explored valleys through the fiction stories that she had taught herself to read. It became her drug.

An older woman who had taken it upon herself to take Malaika under her wing came to visit at school bearing gifts. She counselled the girl, showed her affection, and love, plus gave her a listening ear every time they had sessions.

These sessions were once every two weeks. Malaika was taught how to write down her feelings, her fears and to also celebrate her joys in writing

They would pray together and slowly Malaika gained her self esteem.

She started participating in things she would not have done before. Music, song, drama, and writing had become her extra-curricular activities while in boarding school.

Her secret life at school bloomed, but everytime she went back home for school break, she would sink low.

Mother was still the same.

Malaika who now had a voice as an older girl in highschool started talking back every time mother got a stick to hit her.

In the previous years Malaika would let her just hit anywhere; head, back, hand, or rain blows.

As a girl in her mid and late teens Malaika started taking cover with her hands to protect parts of her face, and head.

Instead the thick sticks would end on her wrists. She always had scars on her wrists and hands from protecting herself. She began to care less as every letter of apology she wrote to mother fell on deaf ears.

What confused Malaika was that the way mother treated her was far different from the other children she had borne.

At this point Malaika started questioning her existence in the home, in the world, and her identity, as life became useless.

In her mid years while in junior high school she attempted suicide for the second time.

This time while on a break from school.

She swallowed a handful of pills. In the silence of her room.

Funnily enough mother decided to send her to the nearest store just a few minutes after the ordeal.

"Malaika, come buy some groundnut paste from the shop, quickly, " shouted mother.

In fear she could not say she wasn't in a position to go there. Malaika thought "mother can not know I swallowed all those pills I had kept in my suitcase from the nurse at school."

The walk to the nearest store seemed like a trek to oblivion. She started sweating profusely. Her legs got weak and could not carry her until she sat by the roadside on the tall grass.

Tears voluntarily plopped down her face. She tried to call for help to anyone who could hear but no one came by. She felt helpless knowing her legs could not move, her heart palpitated with a vengeance. During those days the school nurse would give medication with written instructions on how to take it.

Malaika always finished her dose.

Then there was medication you had to bring from home in case you got ill and the school-store had run down. So that's what she had tried to kill herself with; an assortment of medicine.

If you saw the effects they had on her as she half sat, half lay crying on the ground while dragging herself back from the shop, wishing that death would take her quickly; to bury her plus her sorrow. She waited. It never came.

Malaika realized the longer she stayed there, things would be worse because mother never liked her delays on errands. So in fear and confusion torn between wanting to die and return home quickly, before mother noticed her delay, she dragged herself to her feet.

Malaika thought if she tried to gag by putting her fingers down her throat, the medication would come out and she would stop feeling drowsy and drugged.

All in vain.

She cried once again cursing at God for having her suffer like this. That night she cried herself into delirium and a stupor until sleep took her. She ended up tossing and turning, having nightmare after nightmare.

***

Rattling around in the labyrinth of my brain

Meandering corridors leading to rooms filled

with moments frozen in memory each significant

In the influence it has had by

remembering reinforced by recalling

***

Malaika outgrew her teens. She had lots of trouble concentrating in class and was always in and out of hospital with some illness, because her immunity was rather low.

She learnt to block the depression at school by always helping others. Before long whoever needed to talk about anything from boys to parents, to friendships gone sour, came looking for her for advice.

She found herself counseling others in boarding school.

At times she was even able to spot someone unhappy or depressed. This gave her a new sense of direction and purpose. She started living again. In boarding school she made all sorts of friends. And in the village she talked to everyone. Always a smile on her face.

School had been hard to comprehend. Until luck knocked her door and a daughter from another mother came to do an internship at her school. They would take time together just dissecting lesson after lesson. Until it all became clear. After years of trying and trying with failure and repeating class after class, making her a grandmother of the class, she started to succeed. She was always older than her mates.

Her dream was to be the best writer in the school. To go for many writing excursions and reading competitions. She was even assigned such roles in the compound. She did those proudly. Her patrons trusted her.

In the end, she passed highschool above average with some good grades. It was now time for college.

Malaika had always had many fearful stories of what happened in college.

Every story from HIV AIDS having rampant increase in colleges, sugar daddy and men of affluence getting to hand pick girls in college, lecturer assigning marks out of sexual favours, lesbianism, gays lifestyle and above all boys exchanging girlfriend like they did their shirts.

Her perception of all this information was total fear. She made a decision to buy a ring and put it on as if she was engaged.

What helped is one of her siblings having given her a mobile telephone. Not many students had those. So everyone at the college believed she was given the mobile device by a boyfriend, making her very engaged and already taken. No boy in college premises even dared make a move. She was relieved.

Time span. She made close friends. Always ready to listen and solve a problem here or there.

She had now become independent.

Being away from mother also helped both of them begin to grow towards each other again. However she still had many many questions about her formative years and why mother had treated her that way.

To console herself she had agreed to tell her brain that it was the best way mother expressed her love to her by wanting no mistake, no fault, all perfection. So mother just did what she knew, and that was to beat her. She was beaten and even locked out when mother got too angry, almost into her early twenties. It was an embarrassment for Malaika. She had written apology letters almost half her life by that time, all gone in vain. Mother just never articulated any good in her child because perfection was her standard.

Heading to internship was a great pride for Malaika. Having to interact with others on a professional level was of great joy. She held herself with her esteem having been assigned others under her.

She started making a home for herself. Every time she went into the trading centre or the city. She would buy nice things for herself. It was a whole new journey just of self love.

Mother started reaching out more. Maybe as they say distance makes the heart grow fonder.

Sadly she knew she had missed her mother's love as a child, missed that bonding. She had built that wall of mistrust between a child and mother. She feared her and not a good fear but a bad fear.

When someone hurt her she never trusted that person again. Her heart was very fickle. That's the damage of who Malaika had become. Inside her heart was dead.

She travelled to remove the loneliness. She made friends to put a smile on her face. She did some wild excursions just to remove a pain that bled in her soul every time she got nightmares, flashbacks. Inside her was a brewing pain that no one and nothing could take away.

She would have episodes of break down and get into depression. Occasionally it would be bad not even allowing her to go to work.

With age she had become an expert in sensing the signs and symptoms. So she would divert all her energy on just waking up every day and chanting to herself " I will be ok, I can do it"

They would say she was so brave but many times the bravest were the weakest people. In her moments of weakness and fear which would just overcome her body occasionally you actually get to know the truth. The little girl inside her was the weakest and most traumatised.

Every time she won the battle inside her.

***

Eleanor Rigby doesn't have the market cornered on masks

I have several myself

Though I do not keep any of them in jars by the door

Mine are on display on various social media pages

They are called profiles instead of masks

They are but a small slice of who I really am

They are the face we allow the public to see

Not always a stranger that we hide from ourselves

I know very well the face I hide from others

No one needs to see it

I have grown quite versatile at transforming

And rarely do I drop the pretense

On the rare occasion that I am

Caught off guard and my bare face is hanging out

I've discovered no one really wants to see it,

They don't want to face themselves

As seen through the mirrors of my eyes

Through slits in a disguise.

***

One of the many jobs she acquired out of her domain got her in close contact with the cruelty of men in the corporate world. She saw how girls gave in to sexual favours just for their job security. It was disgusting.

How people would squander supplies. One of her workmates even told her , " if you don't carry home the leftover supplies. The boss will realise that I have been stealing. So if you don't do it. Give them to me. Malaika you have to do it. I will tell the others you want to spoil our deal "

It was so unfulfilling even if she wanted to give it her best and wanted to learn.

What broke the camel's back was when the one who everyone in the company reported to and who Malaika had been put directly under him to help me with his daily simple office duties approached her in a very unbecoming way.

Being the muscular built man that he was and had been used to women falling at his feet especially that he was of different origin. He had the money moved in very affluent circles, women knew he was their ticket to fame and wealth and so they flooded day in and out of his office. Unashamedly even after knowing he was a married man. They didn't care.

Meanwhile Malaika, being his assistant, watched every time as women came and went out of his office. She felt even worse when the wife popped in to visit her husband. What a life.

Malaika was beginning to weigh her options at the company. When unfortunately. The married boss who had women falling around his feet came to her office next door one afternoon. It was not out of the ordinary. He always did that if he wanted something to be done and he didn't want to use his extension phone or just wanted to supervise what was going around.

So when he entered. Malaika looked up at him eagerly waiting for instructions from him. He surprised her because in a split second he had bent down to kiss her lips. Out of shock she stood up and pushed him aside as he attempted to reach out again. He had a very sinister look, a greedy look like he was ready to jump for his kill. Being a well built tall man, he was no match for Malaika even in a hundred years. Heart pounding, Malaika went round the table, legs shaking, she knew she had to get out of the room fast before he came close or before anyone from another department found them two in such a position.

She waited when he had moved closer since he didn't intend to stop until he got what he wanted.

As he did so Malaika scuttered under his arms so fast that he was left shocked behind.

When she reached the corridor she reduced her speed so no one would notice her running and be suspicious.

Meanwhile she looked behind her thinking the boss was on her heels. She almost tripped when she saw his shadow. Her brain had stopped functioning but her feet just moved and took her to another department office on the same corridor.

As she entered she had his footsteps cross and go to his office.

Forehead sweating, heart pounding, legs almost collapsing under her Malaika stopped.

The guys in the room looked up thinking she had come to deliver something from the boss to them, which was a normal occurrence. When they saw nothing in her hands. They cheerfully greeted me. Her mouth was dry. She just shook her head as if to say fine. Pretended to arrange some papers on the photocopier machine. Waiting for a few minutes to see if the boss would come out of his office. When he didn't. She smiled and walked out.

To her disadvantage when doors opened in that corridor there was an echo when people walked down the corridor you would practically hear their footsteps. It was always a nice distraction but on that day she cursed the corridor floor over and over as she tried to tip toe back to her office. Hoping no one stepped out behind to wonder why she was tiptoeing and hoping the boss didn't get out of his office to see her tiptoeing back.

She reached safely eventually. Entered. Sat. Stood. Was shaking as her brain finally registered what had happened.

Her fear now was if the boss decided to call her in his office. She prayed that he didn't because she was not ready to face him then.

She also prayed that time would fly so she would leave the building that day and just take a bath.

When she looked at the clock it was almost time for everyone to disperse.

But when that time reached she wondered how she was going to lock her noise door and alert the boss with all the key jiggle and lock that she was headed out. She tried all in vain to make less noise.

He didn't open his door until she was now on the second flight of stairs. He got out, came to the rails and stood. She almost tripped over when she looked up to find him staring at her as she walked down. Their eyes met, hers in shock with that sinister look. It seemed to say " see you tomorrow."

Malaika could not hold herself; she ran down the remaining stairs.

As she reached the gate she almost wanted to burst because it seemed like since the boss reached down her face for a kiss she had stopped breathing. Now that she was out the gate, her lungs opened up. Her eyes on the brink of tears. She felt abused, disgusting like she had lost trust again in someone. It hurt.

On reaching home. She scrubbed herself more than was necessary in the bath to wash away the events of the day. As she slept at night, well she didn't do much of that either because she was wondering what and how she was going to approach the matter tomorrow. In the wee hours as sleep took over she made a decision to go boldly and speak to her boss face to face and tell him she was not interested in any illicit affairs and she loved her job. That if he was letting her keep her job based on that then she was ready to quit.

Which she did in the mid- morning. She crossed her fingers that she would go to him before he came to her for any jobs that day. She did not want to face him awkwardly as he was assigning her any duty that day. She wanted everything to be on her terms that day. She was ready. All she had to do was wait after he had completed his morning routine of calls, coffee that he liked to do by himself and emails.

One she figured he was done. She walked to his door. Her knock was firm. She entered on his answering " come in. "

She walked in, stood at the door half ajar and told him, " Sir, do you have a moment I would like to talk to you. "

He looked straight into her eyes but she didn't look away. Although inside there was a circus of all feelings but mostly fear.

He noticed her serious look and said, "Close the door and come in "

Now that wasn't the exact scene that had played out in Malaika' brain. In fact she almost laughed and immediately felt like she was going to pee on herself. You see Malaika had once read that on such occasions when you felt in danger never close the door. Yet here was a big muscular built tall military trained man who had kissed his employee and the employee and pushed him and ran off under his arm asking her to close the door and come in.

It was more like walking voluntarily into your slaughterhouse.

When she reached his desk. At this time her brain had already told her the best position was to stand in front of him, so that she would be ready to take flight if he attempted anything.

Instead when she stood he motioned for her to take a seat. Again Malaika was now realising her chances of escape had reduced. She was somehow confident. She had put on a sanitary towel that morning before she left home plus biker pants under her trousers. The old-school trick in the book. Put on a sanitary towel say you are in your menses, on top put on biker pants then trousers which surely are not as easy to remove just in case. In her brain with those weapons as her confidence she sat head held up to his eyes, not flinching but if you looked seriously at the base of her neck you would notice palpitations, and her behind only sat on the edge of that chair.

He had even pushed his laptop aside, looked and was waiting.

In most cases when you entered his office he was too busy to look at and gave instructions with his head bent or hand on the phone covering the mouth piece or something. He never stopped. So now him giving her all his attention kind of threw her off guard forgetting she was the one to begin the conversation. When she realized he was actually waiting. She cleared her throat. Ahem! " Sir according to what happened yesterday in my office"

He interrupted and said, "What happened?"

She looked at him with a look that said " oh! So you want to play that game."

His eyes were actually smiling like it was a very normal conversation they were having over a cup of coffee.

Malaika realized for him to take her seriously, she had to pull up her socks.

She continued now more confidently, looking him directly in his eyes, " Sir, yesterday you came to my office and tried to kiss me. I'm not comfortable with that happening again. I love my job and respect you and I hope my job here will not have to involve you kissing me. I would like to know now if it is so. I can leave with immediate effect."

The man sat up straighter and realized that the girl had not come back for a recap of the event but in real action but that she had come to refute his actions and stand her ground. He fidgeted with his pen.

When Malaika saw this in a way she realized her point had been hit straight home.

He cleared his throat. Put on a smile and said, " Malaika, what happened yesterday will not happen again. Your work is valued."

That is all Malaika heard, the rest of what he said passed from one ear to another. Inside she was shaking with relief.

He dismissed her with a smile. She said thank you and left.

She never told anyone at the office about what happened. Although girls there used to brag about the illicit affairs from the bosses. Malaika thought it disgusting.

Life continued, work continued. There was restructuring and Malaika was laid off.

She felt sad because she had hoped to learn more and gain a lot since she used to admire the corporate world. Then she also knew she was not as skilled, having just got out of college, but in a way she thought it was sad maybe if she had met the boss' needs he would have not put her name on the list of those being asked. As one of the ladies eventually told her. " Aaah! Malaika, are you serious? How do you think we have survived here? Some of us give away some goodies to stay here for years. How foolish you are to be next to the main man and get booted out. You are very naive. "

Malaika asked her, "But you are in a committed relationship and he is a married man?"

She laughed and said, " And so?"

Malaika cried out, very confused, " Aaah!

"Well what we do here remains here, I know he is married but I need my job" she said.

Malaika replied, "Well I think that's very hard for me to do."

"Yes, girl, with your being so nice and holy you will forever remain jobless"

For sure Malaika began a journey of joblessness for months.

An opportunity came knocking when she was asked to go work in her true profession. It took her many kilometers away from home.

***

I'd spent my 20s looking for romantic love, unsuccessfully, and my 30s studying classical voice and exploring my creativity, and growing as a teacher. I was Pollyanna and an idealist! I spent my 40s learning to live alone and accept myself with all my flaws. I really did not want to be alone. I'd spent 15 years living in a sexually confused relationship with a woman I truly loved to avoid loneliness. I did not want to become that old lady who lives down the block that nobody ever sees. I did not want to become that eccentric character, which is what I imagined the single life to be.

Bill was a wonderful part of my life, and the catalyst to my sexual discovery. ...

When life in the basement of the bigtime bookstore came to an end, I once again resorted to prayer. And once again...I was led to the classroom through a dream that answered those prayers.

So now, at 49, I did it again.

And miraculously, the prayers were answered, again... I was hired by the Diocese of Brooklyn's TV Network where I wrote, hosted and produced over 400 live educational programs for junior high students over the next 8 years. I got to flex all my creative talents...wrote and sang theme songs, wrote skits for the students to perform, directed students in those skits and assisted the editor in putting the tapes together. I learned quite a bit about TV production and had the thrill of introducing an animated character to my young audience. Obadiah had his own e-mail address and fan base.

But just as this new career took wing, I lost my Aunt Antoinette and Bill in the same year.

***

Malaika did a few runs here and there within her scope of study. For two years she put all her mind and focus on her career.

Being an adventurous soul she sought to look further geographically. This would bring her closer to her best friend and confidant. The brother to her twin; friends from her childhood. They have always written back and forth to each other by post. He always encouraged her to be her best. For some reason he became a guardian angel to her.

Hami was his name. In kiswahili his name meant defender, protector, supporter, patron, show favor. Like his name he had unconsciously become her life support.

Whenever she felt like she was drowning and suffocating, in fear Malaika would go to him. At some point she even started drawing pictures of their wedding. At that point in her life Malaika had convinced herself that he was her soul mate.

Meanwhile Hami, being the African man that he was, had probably seen a few skirts by then. She was very naive, while he had experience under his sleeve.

Malaika knew he was the one. Hami started warming up to the idea.

A couple of months down the road he became her first. Malaika had waited for this ever since she got out of college. She had dreaded any men or boys but prayed that he would be the one to unveil her.

They became a couple. Living and working away from each other but they did try to make it work. Hami almost venerated on the ground she walked. She was young and pretty brave.

His mother even suggested he take a "bride price" to seek Malaika' hand in marriage. Hami' mother had seen this girl grow from a tender age going by her home every school morning and she adored Malaika.

Hami was a handsome man, educated, had a great paying job, and women would throw themselves all over him.

One of the twins had a wedding. Hami had to give away his sister and Malaika was present for her best friend's wedding. It brought forth many schoolmates of the twins and Malaika. Old and new friends gathered. They celebrated and danced. Every time Hami would turn around and wink to Malaika as if telling her he could not wait for their day.

The bridal entourage was called for a dance with the newlyweds. The rest of the guests joined in all excited. As people danced, shaking their shoulders and behinds the

African way. Someone whispered to Malaika that Hami' ex- girlfriend had also come for the wedding. It's as if all the doubt Malaika slapped her right in the face. Hami had many times excused himself to receive his calls away from her; she had suspected he had another woman in his life.

Malaika looked at the now ex- girlfriend, she looked beautiful and confident, and his age and for some reason Malaika was jealous.

So she marched with a scowl on her face to Hami and whispered, "We need to talk"

Hami followed her and they ended up in one of the rooms.

When they got there. She barked at him, "Why didn't you tell me your girlfriend was here!"

He was staring at her and almost lost balance, he had never seen her this angry.

He replied, "Girlfriend? I'm confused, you are my girlfriend"

Hami always liked making silly jokes. So when he saw she was not flinching to his answer. He changed his tone.

"Yes darling, I invited you!! How could I come to my sister's wedding, your best friend and not invite you," smiling with a twinkle in his eye.

She barked angrily stamping her feet, "Hami I'm serious. Stop joking, your ex- girlfriend is here, why didn't you tell me"

He stopped smiling, "Darling I didn't know she was coming, she is a friend to the family, I'm sorry, you are the girl I got"

Just like that Malaika melted. He always had a way with her. Having a friendship since Malaika was 10 years, Malaika a fully grown woman now shy into her thirty'. His smile melted her, the gap between his teeth well that just brightened her day.

They kissed and made up like they always did after every fight in her adult life. Immediately joined the rest of the company to continue the celebration. That day everyone in Hami' extended family met Malaika. Some even started calling her daughter- in- law. One old woman was so excited she told Hami she was expecting grandchildren soon.

That sealed Malaika' doubts.

As they parted to head to their separate work places, life went back to normal.

Malaika began to notice that Hami' was not taking things seriously. He was content and knew many people and companies. Malaika asked him to help connect her to get a job in the same city as him, he brushed it off. He started getting bored about the relationship and not putting in the effort to make the long-distance relationship survive. He stopped making calls as usual and when he did he had a fault or the other to nag about. Again Malaika suspected he was seeing another woman. She became discouraged. Verbal fights became the norm. One thing led to another and when one day Malaika threatened not to answer his calls just to spite him and see if he would change. Hami actually cut off their connection and refused to speak to her completely.

Now for Malaika this was devastating. You see. A couple of years ago, before Hami had gone to Malaika' home with a hope to seek a blessing for marriage. Malaika's father and mother had quizzed him. He was confident they looked pleased. However after he left mother firmly forbade Malaika to see him "the boy" in her words.

She had wept for days, and lost appetite to eat for days. Lost weight. Those in the home had never seen her this way. They were worried.

Their paths crossed again after this break and now that Hami was shutting her out voluntarily, she was heart broken.

Back to the present. You see initially Malaika had told herself out of anger that if she stopped talking to him. He would come to his senses and start being serious and commit to the relationship. She even told herself since mother had refuted their union, maybe she was right. So she told herself she would give him a couple of days to make up his mind to commit. After the days she hoped elapsed with no word from him. Malaika got unsettled. She called and he refused to pick. Her messages were all sent with no response. Malaika even asked one of her girlfriends to intervene and talk to him on her behalf. He picked her calls but said he was done.

***

Each day I fade a little more
Energy replete, non-existent
Each day I replace the mask
Don the persona that most expect

Each day I sleep a little longer
Move a little slower
Take a little longer
Accomplish a little less
(Sometimes a little more)

Each day I run through the rat's maze
That has become my mind
My obsession
My anxiety
I am in the habit of it
The habit of fretting
The habit of powerlessness
The habit of pollyanna
That continues to believe there is still
Somewhere
Inside me
A phoenix that will rise

I am waiting

I am tired

Every day I fade a little.

I am afraid

***

It took her almost half of that year buried in her anguish and despair of having to lose not just the love of her life but her guardian angel, her confidant, her best friend.

They say to get over a man you need to get under another. So Malaika went on a rampage. On her forehead almost an invisible tattoo that said, "I'm a survivor; I can do heartbreaks." She did not give a damn about who or feelings. She actually didn't care anymore. Her heart became as cold as ice.

Being geographically inaccessible to the city social amenities didn't deter her from getting on a bus over the weekends to go have fun.

She would take herself to a hotel, book a room for herself, go to the movies, jump on a bus to sightsee; all these activities she did alone since she knew all that men wanted was to get inside her skirts. She dated guys but would leave them hanging anytime they got close. To her they were like a plant; good to look at, but with thorns that could pierce. She became fierce.

Then to cover up her pain, she buried herself in writing all over the place. You see Malaika had learnt to use what new technology called social media. One would communicate and meet people from all corners of the world. That's how she joined a writing platform. Her works got recognized and published across the seas. The editors and publishers were wonderful people who she had never met but talked to through her writing platform. One of the editors took on Malaika' anthology of work that she had written and compiled together with her apprentices and it was published. Unfortunately bless her soul, the wonderful editor later succumbed to an illness. Without even knowing this editor had brought so much hope, lightness to a dead soul Malaika.

Malaika began to live again. The pain slipping away with every achievement at her work place. She had acquired a name in the locality and district. All her apprentices made it with flying colors. Bringing many to wonder who was behind it all. To the point that there were malicious people around the locality who wanted to tarnish her name but all efforts failed. God was always on her side.

Along her social media writing one gentleman noticed her writing and approached her for an offer to do a writing about him. You see he had a story which he needed to tell the world through writing. He wanted to publish an autobiography.

This intrigued Malaika.

But as always with determination she was ready for a challenge.
***

While training my instrument I was working, at the now defunct, Harcourt Brace Jovanovich Bookstore on 48th Street and Third Avenue in Manhattan. I got quite an education from my colleagues in "The Basement of the Big Time Bookstore"- the working title of a musical I was inspired to write with David Henderson, another bookstore employee, after the store closed. I wrote 12 songs based on David's outline and that's about as far as we got.

What did I learn? It was like living in a library/think-tank. Unpublished aspiring writers, actors, painters, singers and musicians were my colleagues. And each taught me something about their talents and aspirations and how vital to life it was to use that talent. And they all pointed me to their role-models; a fertile resource for the creative arts, and a wonderful energy to be surrounded by all day long.

I read more books at that time than I read in all my college classes. I learned about the "Beats" and Ginsberg and Jack Kerouac. About Hunter Thompson and Tom Wolfe... About Helmut Newton and "Pat the Bunny"... About Shel Silverstein and Maurice Sendak.

I'd fallen in love with literature and in particular poetry when I was in High School. It was all reborn again at HBJ. I had written poetry before, but I resumed writing it then. I also started a Journal; an interesting device for self-reflection; not sure if it would have anything significance for future generations. The Point is- creativity is contagious. Teaching is exciting others about things that excite you. Excitement is contagious. A good teacher makes learning exciting and contagious.

And then I started teaching 8th grade at St. Adalbert School in Elmhurst, and my real education began.

Doctors take the Hippocratic Oath, "Above all, do no harm." As a teacher, you are in charge of the minds, both intellectually and psychologically, and so I always prayed that I would do no harm to my students psychologically ever. That I would reflect back to them, and expect from them, the best that they could be, and reinforce that as much as possible. My hope was always to inspire and challenge and encourage my students, especially at this major transition point in their lives, to be excited and prepared for the future. I love 13 year olds. The years a person is going through puberty are as radical and full of enormous physical changes, including in the brain, as the first few years of life are. This I know not only as a result of formal learning, but from my own life experience as well; I would come back after Christmas break, and my students would all seem to have grown right before my eyes.

The only constant in life is that things change.

Transitions in life are not always easy to negotiate. But they can be exciting and not so scary, if you have support along the way.

***

Zuberi is very cheerful. That was the first thing she noticed. And his name captured a lot of attention, it meant one who is strong.

Very inquisitive to know the story behind the scars on his body.

So she started taking record of every conversation they had. With the intention to gather as much information to write his story as he had requested.

They had specific days during the week when they would take stock of as much information. It was not easy for either party. The narrator almost had to relive the shadows of his past ghosts and pain, the writer unknowingly had to capture the dark moments.

It took months of back and forth telephone conversations plus texts.

Unknowingly a friendship brewed. Beneath the mask of pain, they drew much closer to each other.

Malaika was beginning to let her guard down and a client began to pursue her. She let it flow. At the crossroads of no turning back. They both agreed to dive deeper since they were both single and unattached.

Malaika started laughing a lot, silly smiles across her face every time she was attending to her apprentices. One time her colleague even told her she looked brighter. Truth to the fact she felt something she had not felt in a long long time and maybe never.

In truth Hami had been a representation of her innocence, her pain, her safe place.
This that she was experiencing with Zuberi was a new dawn, of freedom, of bravery.
It was a whirlwind of romance.

***

THE THUNDERBOLT

He was bald,
but with a tattoo on the back of his neck,
and on his ear.

He had facial hair that changed
each time I saw him.
Sometimes a beard,
then mutton chops,
then a beard and no mustache,
then a mustache and no beard.

He may not have had hair on his head,
but he was very creative with the hair he had
on his face.
And he had green eyes that twinkled.
That was the cincher.
I was struck by the proverbial,
as they said in "The Godfather",
Sicilian thunderbolt.

I was mesmerized

***

To get her facts and data collection. Malaika took to travelling. Met and had a few questions for Zuberi.

The story started unfolding layer by layer. The meaning of every scar getting visible in her mind by the day. He had undergone the knife on several occasions as a child. It was traumatic. For him to have survived such an ordeal and come out strong. That was another story. She met members of his family while carrying on with her assignment.

As days turned to months she fell in love with the person in him, she started imagining a world full of greatness and strength with them together.

One fateful day as she travelled from the rural workplace to the city, Malaika who normally used motorbike as a common means of transportation got involved in an accident. Her favorite "customer" bike rider who did many of these errands with her since these were over forty minutes rides and more hit a rock and in the split of a second Malaika was flying off the back of a speeding bike hit the ground bearing no helmet. As pedestrians and vehicles stopped to help. All she could think of was her handbag with money and her ATM card. In some areas it was known that during an accident some people didn't run to the scene to help but to steal from the injured.

.

As Malaika lay there in shock head down on the stoney road all she whispered painfully to Omondi the bike man before she passed out in shock. " Tafadhali shika kibeti yangu mtu nisiibiwe", please hold my purse no one should steal from me.

Omondi did just that. She came to realize she was at the rural hospital. Omondi was at her side clutching onto her bag like his life depended on it. On seeing him, she smiled but with loads of pain all over her body. She had sustained bruises and bumps. The wounds had been cleaned and dressed and they scalded like fire all over. Her head pounded like a gong and she had an almost migraine.

The doctor said she was lucky there was no internal bleeding. After a few hours of monitoring. She was discharged. Omondi helped get a taxi ride for her back. Omondi had sacrificed his almost half days earning to be by her side and she now realised why she had put much trust in him. He was a trustworthy and kind person. He promised to go by her work place to check on her the following week and they parted.

On returning back to her quarters where all the employees resided her workmates could not believe how tragic it had been. She stayed since the day had recommended a week's bedrest while she was indoors. Her friend in the compound made some food and brought her.

Now Malaika had to put off writing for a while. She called Zuberi to inform him of her ordeal. He was saddened. He got very concerned and worried. Since Malaika had been down the rural with no relations close by. He insisted he would travel to check on her. Now owing to the fact that he was many towns away and he was a very busy man with business to run alongside being employed this was a big sacrifice.

He jumped on a night bus. Got to the village the following morning. She was shocked he had made it. He stayed during the daytime. They had lots of funny stories to laugh about his journey, his challenges at work and they even cooked lunch, had early dinner and that evening Omondi the " customers" bike rider took Zuberi back to the trading centre to catch a bus back to the city.

That was the day Malaika realised that Zuberi was not joking that he actually cared and loved her like he had always said.

On Zuberi's arrival back to the city he sent a message saying he had reached safely and told her he loved her and wanted her to be his girlfriend. She responded very affirmatively and confidently after seeing how serious he was.

Weeks on end communication grew stronger and they were no longer even talking about the book anymore but sweet nothings with many I love you' in between the day. He had a hectic job which was running a department although he earned a lump sum package. Being that he had survived an injury although lost a lot of body tissue, he could not work and text at the same time. Through all this he was always able to find time to respond and call. To Malaika she needed no other proof. He was kind, loved children so much that on his free days he would be babysitting his siblings' children. He had a great job, he shared the same faith and values with Malaika.

She felt like she had hit the jackpot. He seemed to tick all the qualities of a great partner. During the holidays Malaika would head to the city. Stay with friends and hang out with Zuberi. Everywhere they hang out people thought they were siblings. They looked alike and just had a spark very friendly and welcoming. Of course, people always stared when they heard him addressing her as "babe". The scar tissue always drew a lot of attention, he said people could not imagine he had such a stunning lady.

Malaika never even noticed all that because to her it was about the soul and not the physical.

Months later Malaika was to attend an African gathering of marriage in which mother would be in attendance. Malaika thought it wise to alert them both since they would all be in the same city for an official meeting. Mother was eager and excited. Zuberi was nervous. Malaika was ecstatic for mother to finally meet the man that she was hoping to ask for her hand in marriage.

Malaika told mother beforehand that Zuberi had been involved in a catastrophic accident that destroyed everything and left him with severe tissue damage. She even shared some pictures. Mother was thankful that finally she was having a binding moment with her daughter after all the lost years. She even said they would start over. Well in African society marriage had a way to bind even the hardest of hearts.

The plan was for them to meet Zuberi before the day of the function they had come to attend since Zuberi wasn't part of it.

Malaika had told Zuberi to get affordable accommodation for the two they would occupy near the bus station as requested by mother. Mother didn't want to move in the city hustle and bustle.

He sent directions to the place. When they almost got there by taxi, her mother became hysterical. She thought it ghastly and very insecure.

Malaika tried to calm her down and said Zuberi had just done as requested since they had insisted on staying a walkable distance from the bus. Now these lodging boards were next to the bus. Which was logic by then. So when her mother panicked and said she didn't like the place and asked the driver to change and go elsewhere. The next accommodation was a bit distance from the bus. Malaika tried to apologise to mother and even tried to defend Zuberi in his absence but she got too upset. This just made Zuberi nervous on realizing our destination had changed. He sent

Malaika a text message wondering how exactly mother was going to perceive him after that failed attempt. He was very sorry and sent many I'm sorry text messages on his girlfriend's phone.

Once they settled in the new accommodation lodging. The dust settled. Zuberi was to come by after work. The usual rat race many clients in his techie - world to attend to and fix their appliances.

He had promised to leave earlier than usual from his desk. That day was a tense day for him, what with him already blundered with misinformation and miscommunication of accomodations. Later with a mother meeting he didn't even eat lunch.

Malaika had been all day sending him messages to calm him down. She said " once mother sees how happy we are and how serious she will forget, it was miscommunication and people make mistakes, relax"

Zuberi asked her, " are you sure she will like me with all the scar tissue"

Malaika responded, " babe you relax, she saw your picture and she's ok, the journey was long she was tired and worked up, once you get here in the evening all will be ok. Just bring your appetite since I know you have not eaten since we arrived"

Zuberi, " babe you the best, thank you"

***

The Runaway

His favorite place was
and still is
Washington Square Park.
From 1983 to 9/11
you could find him there
any day; riding his bike,
playing frisbee,
one of the many street people/artists
and/or NYU students who hung out
smoking weed and kicking back 40 oz.
of beer at the end of the day.

You could also find him
sleeping in the trees
late at night.
He had a knack
for climbing up there
and finding the branches
that would embrace him
for a night's sleep,
when it would finally come.

Most often he was
an insomniac, and
would finally pass-out
from self-medicating
with beer and whatever other
drugs were available.

He would disappear intermittently
when he could find shelter

in Under 21, or
some homeless shelter, or
some hospital, or
some boy's home
when the truant officer
would find him.
And occasionally,
yet another foster home.

***

He made it in time. As usual, all cheery and smiling. Yeah that smile. It always blew Malaika away.

When she saw him, she stood and waved. Mother and Malaika had been sitting in a place where Malaika would be able to see those who walked into the cafeteria of the boarding lodge they were residing in.

He waved back and walked confidently. When he reached, he hugged Malaika since they had not seen each other for a couple of weeks. Then he stood in front of mother, hands straight to extend a greeting the African way. Mother shook his hand, Malaika introduced him formally, with respect to mother. Once again he extended his polite greetings and told mother he was happy to meet her. With remorse on his face he apologized full of respect about the mishap earlier about the accommodation mother disapproved of. He said Malaika had insisted on accommodation next to the bus and that was the best he could get.

Throughout all their exchange from beginning to end even as they continued to share a cup of tea. Malaika could read the undertones in mother's body language. It screamed mother's disapproval of Zuberi.

Malaika hoped against all hope that Zuberi had not picked any of those vibes. By the time he was leaving and saying goodbye, mother had been reduced to one word responses.

Malaika requested to escort him to the exit. When they were at the gate Malaika' heart collapsed when Zuberi turned and told her, " babe I could tell mother didn't approve of me"

Malaika, " babe it's ok, she will get used to you slowly, give her time."

To her dismay on returning to the table she found mother fuming and very very annoyed.

"Malaika, no!"

She totally refused.

Malaika, "But mother I told you he had an accident you knew it. It was a long time ago."

Malaika tried to argue that she didn't love the physical but the heart. But mother was in so much shock she didn't want to hear anything. They had a heated argument way into the boarding rooms.

At some point Malaika was bitter and crying. She said, "mother you remember some years ago Hami came to visit with intentions for my hand you rejected him now I met this guy I love him, he loves me and you are only looking at his physical why are you not doing this"

Malaika stomped out their room and went out for fresh air, tears flooding down her face and heart like it had been stabbed deep with a dagger.

It was so painful that they didn't talk much. The marriage ceremony they had come to attend in the city of their friends was a rather sombre one. They didn't even sit together.

Meanwhile Zuberi kept texting and calling to find out if Malaika was okay. The night before he had called her and she picked up the phone while crying.

He had told her things would be okay.
She had told him mother just needed time to get used to them being together.

***

ON LOVE

The most written about,
spoken about,
sung about,
acted out,
imagined about,
speculated about,
painted and sculpted about,
influential, life affecting and affirming
emotion,
feeling, and/or action
is LOVE.

Nations have gone to war,
kings have lost their thrones,
treaties have been signed,
and an entire religion was created
over love affairs.

Helen of Troy is proclaimed to have had a
face
that launched a thousand ships.
Edward the VIII abdicated the throne of
England,
"For the woman I love."
Henry VIII created the Anglican Church
and broke with Rome
over his libido and Anne Boleyn.

Antony had his Cleopatra,
but so did Caesar.

Helen had her Paris.
Romeo had his Juliet,
and Ralph Cramden had his Alice.

From Adam and Eve,
down through the millennia
love has been the root of all evil.
After all, God expelled man
from the Garden of Eden
not because they ate the fruit.
But because in eating the fruit
their act of disobedience
was NOT an act of LOVE
for the Father.

All God asked was for love,
freely and unconditionally given,
demanding in return that we trust Him
and rely upon Him
and have faith in Him.

But man was... curious...
hence the Fall.
But in the end
love still saves us all.

***

The day after the wedding. Zuberi came to the bus station to wish mother a safe journey back. Malaika had a meeting as well before she caught her bus. Zuberi agreed to escort her. Later that day as Malaika took the journey back to her work place many towns away she meditated over the whole weekend events and thought to herself. Mother would warm up to her boyfriend eventually.

As weeks turned to months of insults, phone calls and near banishment from those she loved and hoped they would see her point of view. Malaika decided to shut out all the noise just so she would focus on building herself and the relationship she had.

Mother and father were so terrified that they made her cousin travel many towns to speak sense into Malaika. They said she was rushing into marriage.

When her cousin arrived they had a lovely time. They spoke. Malaika opened up and told her she would stand her ground. She would not relent.

These were several weeks after mother had left. Malaika had even travelled to the city to spend time with Zuberi. They had talked about their future and even finally consummated their relationship.

Malaika had never wanted to be on contraceptives. She had heard of terrible side effects. They had chosen to wait. She knew very well that it was very likely that they would conceive.

So by the time her cousin came with a message from mother and father. Unknowingly Malaika was already with child.

Although it had not seriously crossed her mind until after cousin travelled back and a heavy flu persisted. Malaika went to the nearest pharmacy with Omondi, the commuter biker for hire, and she bought a pregnancy kit.

She was excited and eager.

She thought it would be a beautiful blessing for Zuberi and her.

She read instructions on the tiny packet.

Now being in the village had its quirks and qualms. Meaning if you destroyed something you had purchased you had to travel back many kilometers by bike or bus to repurchase.

Since Malaika wasn't taking such chances. She had only bought one kit out of excitement. She could not waste it or take the test badly.

She thought and thought. Till she decided that the best was to get a trough and urinate in it. After dipping the little stick in it and putting it aside to wait. The other alternative was to sit on a toilet bowl and take a piss on the stick but she wondered what if she got too nervous and dropped it in the toilet bowl. Well her first option had seemed best.

Just as she had imagined and hoped. The two tiny stripes confirming her pregnancy appeared like little halos.

It was the best two lines she had ever seen in her life. There and then she screamed and screamed in her wooden house quarters only to find herself flat on her behind down on the floor fallen out of excitement.

At thirty something years Malaika' body had started preparing for motherhood.

That day was the happiest. She held her belly and danced around. It's like all the sorrow that had ever existed in her body, soul was immediately replaced with a glow and a smile.

She even ate for two that lunch hour. She promised the tiny tot growing in her that she would do everything in her power to protect it. She imagined it would be a boy or girl.

That night she could not wait for Zuberi to get home so she could call him with the good news.

When she did finally get a hold of him, she told him.

" I have a surprise! Guess?"

He tried to guess everything but he couldn't.

She laughed louder with every wrong guess he made.

Finally she spared him the anxiety and told him, " I'm pregnant Zuberi!! "

He screamed and laughed and was very excited about the news.

That evening they sure felt the distance. Both wished they would hug each other. But consoled each other with a long long conversation on what the future would be like. Bright.

***

HAPPY BIRTHDAY, MY LOVE

Happy Birthday
Happy Birthday

I love you, a bushel and a peck
a bushel and a peck and
a hug around the neck
oh you make my heart a wreck!!!!

I love your laugh
especially when Max is around
I love your passion when we watch the UFC

I love your strut
I love your butt....haha

I love the expansion of your soul into
everything you do

I love that in making your dream come true
You made mine alive

I love the way you challenge me
I love the way you push on in the face of
anything
I love your stubborn fight for right

I love the way you expand into a room
And I love the power you command

I love you...just you...always

***

TWO YEARS PRIOR.

Malaika being an adventurous one had travelled a lot, met good, cruel and just heartless people. She was an open book pure in heart loving and giving. She understood that people did things out of proportion. Like a while back before she was pregnant, one of her hosts had thrown her out of her house in the evening. She had been looking for a safe and convenient house to move into for days in vain. The night she was asked to kindly move out. Having nowhere to go Malaika called a head of youth at a local church who helped connect her to a young college going lady (Anyango) from the same church. This young lady invited her to share her bed. They would take turns on the bed every other day with the other person sleeping on the floor. They were roommates for months.

Getting cheap accommodation near her workplace had proved hard. At some point she had almost given up and needed a much needed solution. They were now three ladies sharing one room because Anyango' friend was stranded and needed a roof . All the vacant rooms were too expensive. Among the three ladies since she was working Malaika thought it wise to move out .

The cheapest houses were in the outskirts of town. So once again Malaika went to introduce herself to the lady Zuleika who had converted to christianity(a workmate that lived in the outskirts). She told Malaika not to worry that they would go together and look up the accommodation after work. Zuleika owned a beautiful bungalow still under expansion on the highway along Mombasa road. Zuleika had suggested that if Malaika didn't get a house that evening. She was welcome to stay with them till something came up.

Fortunately when they reached Zuleika' locality she made calls and a two roomed house was found. The landlord said the house was available but still needed some finishing touches. Construction had stopped because he had run out of money. So he suggested she pay a two month deposit so they could finish the house in three weeks. In the meantime Zuleika welcomed Malaika to stay at her home.

Malaika was moved by this stranger's kindness. Zuleika was a courageous woman. Her husband being Muslim and not wanting anything to do with christianity didn't want any sign or talk of church. Although he worked in another big town and only travelled to his family every other week.

Zuleika still went to church. She drove herself to night prayers. Malaika was always awestruck at how every time Zuleika entered her doorstep she would pray fervently thankful to God for her day and safe drive back. She prayed over her husband and children. Malaika lived with them for the weeks in which her rental room was being completed. From these two experiences Malaika learnt much about generosity, loving unconditionally and just laughing at the simplicity of life from these two ladies, Anyango and Zuleika.

They developed a routine once Malaika moved out. In the morning Malaika jumped on a commuter and in the evening if Zuleika was going straight home she would give Malaika a ride back. In return Malaika loved playing with Zuleika' little daughter Salma.
Once in a while Anyango would hang out with Malaika after church on Sundays. They loved this time together. Malaika enjoyed buying them treats since by then she had worked for two months at the company. Her work involved numbers. Malaika didn't much enjoy crunching numbers. So when she got an opportunity to go be in charge of some apprentices she grabbed the chance with loads

of joy. It paid more and she saved a lot since they provided meals and accommodation to all the workers. That's how Malaika had ended up working in the village and meeting Zuberi among her adventure trips.

Now being pregnant was blissful but being pregnant in the village had its challenges with transportation to the hospital for antenatal checks and the market to get a refill of her cravings.

The people in the rural area were kind and very respectful since their children were her apprentices. Once in a while the non-resident apprentices would bring from their parents farm produce to Malaika after harvest as gifts. The residents would insist on their guardians meeting Malaika. They loved Malaika and the way she listened to and counselled them. Many of them being orphaned.

Once they noticed her growing with a child, her store was never dry.

These apprentices had a female in charge who would cater for all their needs while in school. She was paid to do that. A retired midwife and very motherly. Elderly but agile. Malaika adored this elderly lady, she was more than a workmate, everyone called her Matty. She had welcomed Malaika to the village. They had even stayed together for a couple of weeks as Malaika' house was being painted and locks being fixed with a few renovations. She became a daughter to Matty.

So when Malaika had discovered she was with child. Matty had been the first one to be told among her workmates. Matty was thrilled. For Malaika it took away all the emptiness that had come with mother's rejection of her pregnancy.

In African culture getting a child out of wedlock was a taboo. A man was to take a "bride price" at some point during courtship. Malaika had no hope for that happening to her, since her parents never approved her relationship with Zuberi.

Matty unconsciously and dutifully took over the mother position in Malaika' life. The morning sickness, the dizziness spells, the raging hormones, the ever growing body and cravings all became bearable with Matty present. Her house was a few blocks away from Malaika but even in the night Matty would call just so she would say good night. Everytime Matty went to the market kilometers away on Onyango' motorbike she would come back with rare fruits for her grandchild as she liked to say.

As time went on Malaika' noticed that Zuberi didn't send money for hospital visits or upkeep as an expectant father should. On the other hand Malaika didn't know how to ask for money. In her head she thought the man was to do it because that was his responsibility to his woman.

Malaika had discussed this with Matty and the elder woman had said, "not all men know how to approach marriage and because you never tell him. He is green to these things. Don't worry, keep telling him."

This bothered Malaika asking money from a man. She asked till got so bothered and stopped. Malaika had a good salary and so she just stopped asking. However he always called daily. He was thrilled to be a father.

Once Matty had told her, "well now that you know your man is the youngest child at home and he is used to being done for stuff he isn't aware that he has to step up and take up a challenge. I think it is wise if you start saving a big chunk of your money for a rainy day now that you have my grandchild coming soon."

Matty went on and said, " marriage doesn't come easy. Don't look at other marriages out there and want to
copy those. Every marriage needs work everyday. Know each other's strengths and weaknesses and build each other."

This was a foreseen step up challenge for Malaika for her and her soon to be family; she had to make it work.
Being in a rural setting near the lake meant that one was prone to malaria every other month. With severe relapses. Maternal child death rate is high.

Malaika weighed her options and a couple of months to the year end she wrote her resignation letter.

Malaika figured that Zuberi was a bit laid back on provision because she was far from him. She thought if she moved closer and got work closer he would be a hands on dad. So as the year was ending a few weeks into the baby's arrival Malaika moved to the city. Zuberi was happy and Malaika realized this was what was missing in the question. Her physical presence.

He came to pick her from the city bus station and Matty arranged for her things to be put on a bus safely a few weeks after to be delivered to the city.

The two parents began another chapter to their lives together in one house. Remember they had never lived together before it was all new to both. Learning each other more, getting acquainted with the good and the not so good.

**

Ah, youth!
Comfortable on your safe secure throne
built on a foundation of love and support
of family and friends

Ah, Youth!
So outspoken and judgmental
trying to appear sophisticated and wise

Wisdom does not come that way

And rarely to the young

It comes from life experience that has been
paid for

with spiritual coin... a toll on your soul...

Ah, Youth!

Be arrogant! May you be able to always be
that arrogant!

May you never know illness,

May you never know loss,

May you never know immobilizing
heartache...

May you never lose the foundation of home,
shelter, food or clothing

May you never need to go to a food pantry or
NYC Human Resources

May you always have your health

And your livelihood.....

May God bless you always and all ways

Ah, Youth!

You have a right to much hope,

but not the right to such judgmentalism and conceit...

But then again....life will teach you what you need to know

And you will learn about the price tag and the bill that will come due.

And when you can still get up and give back... then you can judge, maybe... but you won't

because that is for God to do,

and not Youth

***

Ripe with a child, raging hormones and very flawlessly beautiful those were some of the things she discovered in that season about herself.

Zuberi had been co-renting an apartment in one of suburban locations very convenient to the city. So when Malaika joined them it was only natural for them to fall back on the domestic set-up unlike the bachelor life they had been used to.

She cooked, cleaned and made the place look homely. In the back of her mind knowing soon they had to part ways and start their own life with a newborn. However as time passed by, Zuberi looked like he wasn't going to bring up the issue of them finding their own space for the new family to be.

Once when Malaika was brave enough she brought the subject up insisting she didn't mind even if they moved to a bedsitter so long as they had their own place to bring up the baby and start afresh. Zuberi refused to talk about it. As time went on, she told him they needed to do a lot of baby shopping, he didn't respond and even looked like he was not happy with her bothering him. So Malaika just decided to start buying things everytime she went for nice enjoyable excursions in the city. She had saved for a rainy day.

Everytime she came back with beautiful mini-wears for the little one. At first she would hide the stuff until she realized she had to wash the baby clothes and had no way of hiding them. When he discovered a whole suitcase of baby stuff he was very furious. They had an argument. She blamed him for not caring and he told her she didn't understand.

Before knowing the baby's sex they had always thought they would name the baby Zawadi. After knowing the baby's sex she started searching for an appropriate name. All they knew he had to be named after his paternal grandfather. A first name was yet to be decided on.

Malaika used to have strange cravings during the daytime. Fries, fish, chocolate, ice cream and because Zuberi only left behind money for upkeep feeding. She feared to ask him for money for such cravings. So she ended up budgeting for that from a small savings.

Pregnancy was a bummer while still at her work station, she used to get severe dizzy spells that she would hide from her apprentices. Lie down prostrate in their library room floor with the door firmly closed. Now that she was not working she took evening strolls and in the middle of nowhere she would get dizzy spells. So she tried as much as possible to walk near someone on the road. One day she stopped a stranger and asked him to help her get to her quarters. He held her hand and helped her ahead. With pregnancy she learnt to talk to strangers and realised people were always ready to help a pregnant woman. All this while she never told Zuberi. When she went for her antenatal checks she used to wonder if she would be able to push the baby when time came. She had lots of fear especially after reading of women who died while birthing their young.

Zuberi looked like he was fighting lots of internal battles as time went on but he never opened up to her.

He feared to worry her so he kept it all to himself and tried to act like it was all well. At one point Malaika vomited in the middle of the night he cleaned up all the floor, he always didn't want her bending to wash clothes he wanted to wash clothes over the weekend when he was free but Malaika being bored of being indoors she would do it. She wanted to show him she would be strong for them. He didn't want her pushing herself too much.

On some weekends when he came back early he would take her to stretch her legs down the park. She treasured those moments with him but he never opened up to fully share what was on his mind.

They would talk about everything except him.

Malaika slowly started feeling like she was going through the motions by herself with them not fully connecting. She felt lonely.

It was bad enough for him to have a wall around his heart but even worse for her because mother had totally disowned her. She didn't want to hear anything about her. She missed her mother. She wanted to ask many questions about pregnancy, about giving birth to her mother in vain. However after some time her siblings reached out, her father reached out. They would call to find out how she was. Father once told her to eat fish regularly because it would help with the baby's growth. Her siblings would send her birthday gifts and special messages but it was never the same without that motherly touch from her mother.

Malaika used to get sad sometimes and Zuberi seemed to blame himself and also get downhill everytime he recalled that mother had never acknowledged him.

At one point Malaika just shut all the negatives and decided to live for the life growing in her.

Zuberi' roommate met a lady and they started living together. Meaning however spacious the house was, it had become too small for two women to share a kitchen. Whereas before Malaika had been cooking for the two men and herself, things changed with a new lady in the house. She preferred to cook for her man and she had her budget as per what money he left her. At this point although Malaika had no problem sharing with the new couple, she told Zuberi of her concerns and now insisted it was wise for them to move out and get their own place.

To her surprise Zuberi listened but refused to barge in the decision of them moving out. Not until his roommate told him that his girlfriend preferred them to have a house to themselves.

Malaika didn't take that well and they had a heated argument. She told Zuberi he had refused to listen to her before now the baby was coming very soon and they were going to appear disorganized house hunting at the last minute.

She cooled down after realizing that at least they were going to move into their own place.

She thought they roughly would have a similar budget as what they were going to move out of. So she told Zuberi how she was happy to get her own two bedroom house. Unfortunately Zuberi didn't tell her that he had not financially planned for that. So he kept silent, they looked at several houses, even went as far as the outskirts of town where houses were bigger and cheaper. Malaika, with no knowledge of Zuberi predicament, jumped at every house, excited about color and prospects of them starting over. She was so excited over Zuberi's change of plan that she never noticed his underlying sadness.

Zuberi had lost lots of money on loans when the business he invested in had failed and he had to sell his assets. He was a man, men were not expected to show any weakness in the African set up. He thought he would just keep silent. He let her dream big but never shared a thing of his challenges.

A few days into their house move he could no longer lie to her, he told her , they would not make the move but instead relocate back to his mother's house. His reason being that his mother always nursed all her daughters- in-law after they birthed their newborns and so it would be hard for her to be commuting all the way if they got a house away. Malaika knew that his mother did actually nurse all her daughters- in- law as the African culture required, she had seen her do it. So Malaika didn't suspect anything about Zuberi not fully telling her the truth. So just as they started counting down days to the baby's arrival. Both Malaika and the man who stole her heart ended up at his mother's home.

Once at his mother's home he even appeared more calm.

By that week Malaika had gotten tired of being so heavy. She wobbled like a duck and got angry easily, when they went to church he would tell her to smile and walk properly as she had acquired a limp especially when the baby sat in one position. Zuberi was always sensitive about what the public and his friends saw in them. He always wanted a picture perfect couple. She wanted it too even much more but Zuberi as usual kept so much to himself. She hated it. She even started resenting how he preferred other people's opinions to hers.

It's like a battle was raging underneath as the days drew near.

That last week Malaika went into the baby nesting phase without even knowing. She scrubbed, washed, cleaned, dusted, packed and repacked the baby's things, Zuberi' things. He was not happy every time he came and found she had done a lot of heavy work.

She had also read and done a lot of research about ways of inducing labor while at home.
So she took to massaging pressure points at her feet every time she sat down.

A few nights after as they slept she started feeling extremely hot, tossing and turning. Zuberi looked at her and went to ask his mother to come and check Malaika out.

Mama Zuberi took a minute to look into Malaika' eyes dilated, brows sweating and she said they needed to go to the hospital for a check.

Malaika laughed so hard, she told Mama Zuberi there was no way the baby was coming because her water had not broken and she didn't feel any pain. Mama Zuberi having birthed six children, Zuberi being her last and a couple of grandchildren under her wing, didn't want to frighten Malaika. She gave her a hug and told her it was just for a check up and they would return in case it was a false alarm.

It was a little past midnight and Zuberi called a taxi cab to take them to the hospital.
The nearest one was just a ten minute drive with no traffic at night.

The night shift staff received them, Malaika' heart was pounding and Zuberi was trying his best to be calm for her.

Mother kept distracting them with stories but it was clear they were too nervous to follow. Malaika whispered and told Zuberi she was scared. Then she was called in for a routine check-up by the nurse.

Unfortunately that week the medical staff in the city had all gone on strike so they were short staffed.

The examination had been very uncomfortable, with the nurse checking, poking, pressing.

The nurse confirmed her in labor and already three metres dilated so a hospital admission form was immediately authorised.

Malaika' heart was pounding. As she came from behind the curtains. The nurse told Zuberi and his mother that non-patients were not allowed in the labor ward.

Zuberi asked for a few minutes of privacy with Malaika.

"I'm so scared," Malaika said with a tear in her eyes.

Malaika had read about labor and she was scared and had hoped Zuberi would hold her hand through it all.

"Babe don't worry, you are strong, just do as they ask you, listen to instructions. I will be here in the morning I promise, " said Zuberi.

The nurse, impatiently hovering nearby like she was not amused to be kept waiting, had a pissed off face.

Zuberi kissed Malaika on the cheek, Mama Zuberi hugged her and told her discreetly to be careful.

Mama Zuberi said she was going to call a nurse friend who worked in that hospital to keep an eye on Malaika' well-being.

So Malaika followed the nurse into the labor ward as doors closed behind her, separating her from the known and unknown.

As she walked in, Malaika was shocked at the labor ward. It was a dormitory-like long room with curtains separating each bed.

There were only two nurses moving from bed to bed working with precision and speed attending to women.

Malaika almost laughed out loud because the set up was rather hilarious.

At this point Malaika had no pain or discomfort so she had no idea what was to come.

Some women screamed, others were speaking almost in tongues and other dialects, some were banging on the tables as they held their backs, others writhing in excruciating pain.

Malaika was given a bed and she climbed to sit on it and then tried to sleep but the noise was too destructing, she thought whether she should walk like she had seen a woman down the corridor walking back and forth her clothes almost falling off with abandon as she stopped to hold onto the wall every once in a while. Although the nakedness wasn't something Malaika thought was part of her plan.

Now Malaika had gone to all her antenatal classes and checks but nothing prepared her for what was now in sight.

She could not imagine if she was as strong as all the women in front of her.

As she tried to figure out whether to sit or sleep (she seemed the odd one out not screaming).

From her position on the bed Malaika could peep through her curtain and try to figure out the best posture she could copy from other soon to be mothers (to try and look like a serious patient too) she found herself laughing secretly.

Malaika was getting bored and thought of her and interrupted her sleep that night. She decided to block everything away till the baby was ready to show up.

One of the women whispered to her not to sleep as it would make the baby less active. She encouraged her to walk.

So Malaika tied her kanga around her waist on the kitenge Mama Zuberi had given her that night as they came to hospital. Malaika had no dresses; she had preferred maternity trousers all through her pregnancy.

That night as the world slept, Malaika walked back and forth. Until she got tired of walking and went back to bed.

As she passed by a certain curtain her eyes flew open in shock and her jaw dropped as she saw a mature woman silently birthing her baby by herself. She looked like she knew what she was doing and Malaika could not believe it as she visibly saw the baby's head popping out of the woman's birth canal. Malaika almost fainted but this woman clearly knowing what she was doing kept pushing silently. Out of embarrassment Malaika walked away quickly doubting that the woman even noticed her eavesdropping. As she reached further ahead the nurse passed by rushing to that woman's aid because she had heard the wailing of a baby.

The midwives being short staffed only relied on the sound of these women in the labor ward. With their many years of experience their trained ears would know whose baby was on the way who was far behind. It was a risky affair having just two midwives that night on call owing to the fact that medical personnel were on strike that month.

When the nurse came for a second, follow up, check on Malaika, she said they would have to induce Malaika because she was not progressing in her labor.

So they prepared Malaika, an IV fluid drip pricked into her vein. Being with small veins was a disadvantage because it meant getting many pricks till a visible vein was spotted. It always left her bruised and in pain.

It was as if the IV drip fluid was a silent welcome to the real dance of labor pain. Within minutes Malaika started feeling very very uncomfortable.

She started sweating. Wanted to move but the drip kept her in one position. The nurse probably knew and had taped it securely onto her wrist.

Malaika actually wanted to pluck off the drip because she was now beginning to get irritated with the foreign piece of needle in her body.

Tears started flowing freely down her cheeks. The pain she had seen others writhing over had now migrated to her bed.

Minutes turned to hours and by almost four in the morning Malaika had an increased volume of diabolical innuendos flying from her mouth.

She was exhausted, thirsty, sleepy but everytime she tried to get some sleep another wave of stronger back breaking pain took over her body.

The nurse came and went and by that time Malaika didn't care about what the nurse was upto she just wanted the ordeal to end. They had replaced the empty bottle of IV fluids drip and Malaika was disgusted by it because her wrist had become numb and swollen.

Malaika screamed and prayed out all the prayers she had ever learnt while in catechism classes since she was a little girl, she even sang holy communion songs, probably said a whole service for herself with her as the priest and congregant, Malaika even took on the penance service. She told God to forgive all her sins all that in a child labor screams.

All she needed was a little sleep but that was far from possible. She tried sitting on the floor. She called out to Zuberi to come help her but unfortunately he was nowhere near.

By the wee hours of the morning she was delirious and all her senses were gone. At some point the nurse would check on her but not say a word.

Probably taking into account the remaining time until when the baby would come. At some point she told the nurse she was tired. The nurse told her to be strong and left.

At around 10am the next day, Malaika very weak having lost all sense of direction, she was now breathing weakly very tired but ears very alert.

You see she had known that this hospital had stories and scandals where babies were stolen from their mothers during birth and so even as she writhed in pain she feared if during her weakest time her baby was taken or swapped. Luckily Mama Zuberi had called in her nurse friend to check on Malaika, she was slightly at peace but she could not take the risk and decided no matter what she would keep her ears alert.

At that point the attending medical staff came to examine her and asked her to spread her legs and start pushing. Malaika used all her strength listening out to instructions but it was too hard and her strength had all drained out.

In the same moment because her eyes were closed in defeat but ears alert, Malaika heard many voices enter her curtain space, one person seemed to be explaining and others asking questions. Until Malaika figured it was a group of interns on duty rounds with their professor. She(Malaika) had become a specimen of study among a group of medical students and their professor. The teacher asked questions and the students answered according to what they saw Malaika do. It was rather an embarrassing moment for Malaika to be naked infront of all those people. It was then that the nurse, having given Malaika a little break to gain composure , asked her to push again.

One of the male interns who had been standing next to the bed said, " Malaika push, come on you can do it,"

Malaika could hear their feet scrambling to leave the place, although her eyes were shut tight trying to start push again. In that instant Malaika grabbed the intern's hand(who had spoken to her) and cried aloud, " please don't go, help me push ."

She grabbed onto his hand tight as the medical personnel and the intern beckoned to Malaika, " push, push!"

Malaika gave one big push as she grabbed the intern's hand tight immediately she felt the baby come out of her body, for a second there Malaika passed out.

The intern said, "good job, good job it's a boy, "

She woke up in the split of a second trying to stay awake for the baby not to be stolen, after the baby was placed over her belly as the medical personnel continued with her work down there, stitching and patching up Malaika from second degree wear and tear.

Malaika tried to turn and say thank you to the intern but he was already gone.

Meanwhile she heard the baby's first wail and she knew he was okay. Then she passed out again for a few seconds.

What brought her back to reality was the aggravating excruciating stitching that was being done, Malaika had first felt the injection then the stitches. It was gross more like someone was stitching a piece of cloth and pulling out every stitch. Malaika thought she had experienced "tough" in labor and birth only to realize stitching was by far the worst in the whole miraculous process of child birth.

But as she held her baby boy in a wrap provided by the nurse after his first bath and cleaning, she felt like all the pain had been worth it.

His eyes, his skin, his tiny little fingers, his little nose, his feet it was a sight to behold. She held onto him like her life depended on it, she was enveloped with protectiveness instantly. She lay down on the bed beside the baby trying to sleep but her body full of emotion and overriding endorphins could not sleep. Her baby was born at around 11am.

As she lay down numb from her waist down from all the trauma she tried to feed her baby but didn't know how to do it right. She could not latch the baby right.

He seemed so calm she just let him sleep.

It was then that she noticed new faces around her that hadn't been there the night before.

She greeted the two mothers near her. One she noticed had no baby. She wondered why.

They told Malaika she was lucky to have been stitched immediately. These mothers had delivered earlier but had not been stitched and were waiting. It was then that Malaika realized the friend Mama Zuberi had contacted had actually ensured that Malaika had been overseen and she was grateful.

The mothers told Malaika how they dreaded the stitches they had been waiting for, for hours. Malaika felt very sad and even grieved more when she learnt that the lady who had been carrying no baby was empty handed because her baby had died after birth.

Across from their row of beds was a woman who had birthed but had been bleeding profusely; all her sheets were soaked.

All the mothers nearby were worried about her.

Meanwhile the ward was still understaffed. Malaika could not believe that her little one and her had made it through till then.

Malaika was transferred to the maternity ward where visitors could visit by 1pm.

The walk to the ward was the longest because she had to carry her baby and walk along the corridor but it was as if someone had made a mistake and stitched her legs together just a step was like coals of fire vibrating between her legs. Meanwhile she was expected to follow the nurse who seemed to forget that a few hours ago Malaika had just pushed a human being out of her body. Malaika thought her heartless and she felt like she was in boot camp.

Malaika went to the ward to wait for her visitors and by that time she had texted Zuberi with good news and he had called to assure her that they were on their way.

They reached early but had to wait for visiting hours.

The procedure was to sleep in for one night for observation and then head home the next day.

Zuberi and the newest grandma, all smiles came in singing jubilation song of praise. The African way in the local dialect, she was overjoyed even though she had other grandchildren but this one, you could tell was special because he was the baby of her baby(her last born child had got a baby).

Zuberi had brought red roses and you could tell although his eyes were red and exhausted from lack of sleep he was jubilating.

The first thing he looked at were his toes, his fingers and he got so emotional. Touching his own child's fingers were a moment he could not express.

Malaika could see and tell even in the unspoken that he was so proud to be a father.

They passed the baby around, others hugged and parted Zuberi on the back.

Just before they left they prayed over the baby and Malaika. Mama Zuberi and a few of the older women taught Malaika how to latch the baby so he could breastfeed. The doctor also passed by and showed Malaika the easiest way to breastfeed. She felt relieved.

Before leaving the ward every mother had to pass by the immunization room and have the baby get their first jab.
Malaika had noticed that her baby' eyes were not as clear as they should be.

When her turn reached for her baby to receive immunisation and register his name. She told the nurse her concerns. Being understaffed most available personnel were very impatient while attending to patients.

So when Malaika raised her concerns of her baby, the nurse told her, " mama inakaa hautaki kwenda nyumbani leo. (Mother it seems you don't want to go home today)

"Hapana ni vile nimeona hali ya mtoto nikasema nikuambie" (no it's because I saw the baby's condition and I thought I should tell you), said Malaika.

The nurse didn't peep to check his eyes, instead she just gave him his jab and said next!

Malaika literally trekked back to the ward. Her feet still sore and the stitches even more tighter with each step. She could not wait to be picked up later on.

Zuberi arrived at noon with his sister- in - law to pick up Malaika. The drive back was treacherous because as much as his sister-in-law tried to drive carefully and slowly avoiding bumps. Malaika felt like her body was in a total mess and had been torn apart and sliced. The weight of the baby in her arms brought warmth and sunshine to her soul.

As they drove back Malaika started absorbing everything that had happened in the past few days and was a bit heartbroken. On the day they rushed to hospital in labor, it was Mama Zuberi who had paid for the bill.

All this while Malaika had been excusing and brushing off Zuberi' aloofness with the thought that he had been saving up for hospital birth that's why he didn't dig much into his pockets but that day at the maternity hospital it had hit her that he had not saved up. So as they drove home with the baby, Malaika was hit with the reality of it all and she felt betrayed by Zuberi.

They were yet to begin the real phase of parenthood.

**

I go through the motions
That mimic life's illusions
But life is suspended
Seemingly ended

Bad news in the mailbox
On a Friday afternoon
I can hold my breath till
Monday comes, but not too soon.

I am too tired to weep
Too exhausted to sleep
The ache inside so deep
The road ahead is too steep.

Have no idea where to turn
Although others say they have concern
My normal life will never return
At this age what more can I learn?
***

Getting home was beautiful just looking at his little eyes and his little fingers holding tight into her hands was worth all the pain her body and heart felt.

The first week well let's just say was like trying to bite into a bone. Hard. From getting frustrated that not enough milk was being expressed out of her body into the baby's tummy, to not knowing how to bathe him because he seemed so fragile in a baby bath, to her toilet visits and personal hygiene moments post delivery. It's like her body was standing next to her watching and waiting for her to comply with her body. Nothing was clicking into place. Mama Zuberi and her daughter-in-law were always there at every turning moment even when they heard her cough they would run to her side. Her bedside was always full of what to eat and drink. Zuberi' mother woke up at the crack of dawn just to ensure it was just right. Self sacrificing her comfort just to make it easy for Malaika.

She taught her how to have her salt baths. Apparently these were always something to look forward to because they helped soothe the wounds and were easy for stitches to absorb and heal faster.

Now nobody had told Malaika that before birth it was advisable to use the toilet for number one and number two. Obviously she had had number one. So after arriving home with a baby she was obviously eating as much to have enough breast milk supply. She ate from leafy greens to porridge to soups. You can imagine what day two of bowels was like! By day three she was getting into a delirium of panic. She needed to use a toilet for number two but for one she could not imagine where exactly what she needed to was going to pass through. It felt like whoever had stitched her had closed up number two passage. She would go sit on the seat and come out in fear shaking after having done nothing. Malaika had shared this all with Mama Zuberi and so they tried every home remedy for a three day constipated tummy.

By this time Malaika felt the ache pulsating at the top of her head. All the toxins in her body after three days needed to be expelled out.

So they tried a soap enema like it's done for babies. You can't imagine how Malaika cried in the toilet until finally, the elder lady got in the toilet room and told her to stand up and tried out the first aid for herself. She literally got the soap and fixed it in Malaika' number two passage. She didn't have gloves or anything.

Malaika was humbled. She wanted not to be just a daughter-in - law but a daughter -in - love. The first aid didn't work. But eventually after Mama Zuberi made many calls and enquiries, an elderly woman visited and advised them to boil water and let Malaika drink lots of warm water. Within a few minutes it worked. It was such a relief and she literally broke down in tears while sitting on the toilet seat and doing her business after three days of almost losing her mind. Apparently the water was what would loosen the bowel movement.

In between all this, Malaika who had come had been nursing anger about how Zuberi had not saved up for the baby. They withdrew from each other like day and night. They started going downhill in their relationship.

She even requested him not to share a bed with her. To everyone they were the new happy parents but behind closed doors they were fighting non verbally.

She didn't want his help at all. Anytime he came in and tried to help she just pushed him away. Considering her hormonal body with short nights, short blackout (heavy mini- naps) when the baby wasn't crying from colic, and her aching breast from feeding she was so imbalanced to make any sane decisions. Sometimes when the baby cried she would be confused because she didn't know what the baby wanted. Mama Zuberi had told her to be patient because with time she would know the different types of cries.

In all that Zuberi felt lost, pushed aside. Malaika was even sad because she was mad at him yet she loved him so much.

In the next week Malaika noticed that the baby was getting more of the pale in his eyes and was bothered. Those who visited said it would go that it was common in some babies and there was nothing a good morning sunshine would not cure. So she started sitting out with him in the morning after their breakfast and feeding the baby. Recalling that the nurse didn't take it as something serious upon the baby's discharge from hospital after birth.

After a couple of days, Malaika had this strong instinctive feeling to take the baby for a check up at the local health center.

So the cab picked them up at mid morning.

On reaching the clinic, the baby was checked and the nurse exchanged a few rush words with the doctor. She exclaimed, "mama umekua unaweka wapi mtoto?"

"Mother where have you been keeping the child?"

They scribbled a transfer letter quickly telling us the baby was in critical condition and needed to go to the main hospital where they had the best neonatal doctors.

Hit like a lightning bolt, at this sudden turn of events, she became numb to her feet, she lost words.

The nurses probably noticed and asked her who she had come with to the hospital.

Malaika told them that her baby's grandma was outside the room.

They came out and told grandma that it was of utmost importance that the baby was rushed to the hospital.

The cab was called back to drive them almost thirty minutes in the traffic to the city major hospital. At that moment all Malaika saw was her life flash past her, all her mistakes, her pain, her joy, everything, and she could not believe this is how she had got there.

On reaching the busy hospital, heavily crowded at the outpatient emergency section. They increased their walking speed to the nurses station. Not yet in any condition to be rushing up and down, climbing stairs because the stitches she had received were nowhere near healing at that point. Malaika didn't even care so long as the baby was attended to immediately.

Malaika handed in the transfer letter and the baby was hurriedly admitted to the neonatal ward.

Which was some floors above the emergency outpatient section

When the baby was received you could see the seriousness of the matter by the way everyone who received him was fast paced. Now in truth Malaika had not understood any medical terms used but she knew it was serious.

Baby was taken into the neonatal room, as the baby cried so hard he was given IV fluids on his tiny wrist, they wrapped his eyes heavily more than once with plaster so his eyes were not exposed and put him under an average size enclosed vacuum with bluish rays, next to him was another baby.

Malaika was asked to sit by him and hold his hands so he didn't pull out the needle attached to his wrist or try to scratch the tape off his eyes.

You have to realize being in a big hospital where everyone generally got affordable services meant limited resources sometimes.
At times it was full capacity that mothers attending to sick babies had to share beds or even sleep on the floor. So long as their babies got a place to lie and receive treatment.

That was Baby and Malaika' reality for the next almost three weeks that followed.

It dawned on her that she had shared a cubicle with three other mothers. There was one bed to sleep on in shifts, a chair that someone had stolen from the corridor where one could sit-sleep.

This new mother became numb, blocking away the pain, hurt, fear, anxiety. In those days she functioned like she was on autopilot. Baby's grandma came early in the morning to drop off breakfast for Malaika, pick any dirty laundry from Malaika and Zuberi passed by In the evening after work.

Friends and family were all praying for the baby, paid numerous visits and offered both emotional and financial help.

One bleak night as Malaika dozed off as she sat on a chair, her head bent down the big bed that had the phototherapy machine where two babies shared the small space. Malaika's baby, unattended by his sleeping mother, woke up, distressed with the needle in his wrist, shook his tiny hand, turning it here and there till the needle slipped off.

The night shift staff would not be amused by it and she would go look for someone to help her return the baby's IV tube back in its needle after it had slipped off with the baby's back and forth sudden movements.

A doctor, not happy by the distress call, came to solve the issue for her, although she warned Malaika to be attentive and keep an eye on baby' wrist.

Malaika would look at the baby and feel sad that the baby, who in his little mind must have been wondering why he was in darkness because his eyes were plastered shut with a big plaster across his face and running downwards from his forehead to the bridge of his nose.

So to break down his little fears she used to talk to him and whisper stories in his ears, she would rub his skin along his arms so he knew she was near him and when he was breastfeeding she would sing him soothing songs.

Baby had a mind of his own because on some days he fought off his IV fluids needle and the nurse reprimanded Malaika. She told her if she can't hold his hand the whole time he is awake then they were to transfer his needle to the side of his head to look for a vein. Malaika had seen the same in another room. This frightened Malaika. So she made a habit of dozing off with his hand held. It also meant no sleep. Every time he shook his arm she would awake frightened that he had removed the tube.

Malaika even noticed there were people who had become permanent hospital residents because of months on end of arrears in hospital bills.

It was just a sad place; babies died every other day leaving Malaika depressed but she never cried. In fact she got aggressive everytime she needed help she just shouted out her needs pertaining to the baby. Other mothers nicknamed her mad mama. She didn't know this until a mother in her cubicle told her and joked about it. "That Malaika was always running after doctors"

The Malaika in hospital had become bold and strong. She learnt that the hospital was a jungle where only the fit survived. So she had to be bold and tough for baby' sake.

At some point this had become exhausting. Between changing staff, doctors coming in and out, baby's going from good to not good. It was like a swinging pendulum.

Every time Zuberi came in Malaika asked him if she could change and go to a private ward where at least she had a chance to sleep or at least to change with someone to help in the day as she got some sleep.

She was bitter when Zuberi didn't see the point. This just drew them at loggerheads. Zuberi obviously had his reasons(financial).

Yet again a silent war in the midst of disillusionment. Baby fighting for his life, his mother having many restless nights, and his father very stressed about how he was going to take care of his young family and keep them safe.

Hami's twin sisters came to visit their childhood friend, Malaika and her baby. Now married mature women, the twins lived in the city, their careers both in the medical field so they came to visit Malaika and also encouraged her to be strong.

They said they would inform Hami (their brother) about Malaika being in hospital with her sick baby.

The next day Hami had come to visit.

He looked like he felt so guilty for having not pursued Malaika many years ago when he had the chance.

Although during their visit his sisters had told Malaika that Hami had recently gotten married. Malaika noticed his ring on his visit at the hospital but she didn't push him further.

***

So I'm out here on this ledge
I look down and my eyes roam over it all
From this precipice that hangs over my life
And wonder what will happen when I fall

My grasp is weakening
My fingers can not hold
They are afflicted with arthritic pain
The price of growing old

There is no safety net
To catch my failing senses
My life's work is buried
Under the debris of life's expenses

Missed appointments with my oncologist
Missed medications from my pharmacist
Bare shelves in my kitchen cabinets
Reveal a truth I am unable to be reconciled
with

I sit devoid of feeling
Numb on my chair
Wondering why I am still here
And why I even still care

***

Malaika had not had actual sleep in weeks. The comfort of a real bed back home and sheets didn't help, she would wake up shivering and in cold sweat from nightmares about all she had witnessed that whole month while back in hospital with baby receiving treatment. Three children had died in her presence. Baby had narrowly survived a major surgery because overnight, literally God had turned his organs to life. A miracle.

One night while still back in the hospital, the baby was to go for surgery and the surgeon didn't show up while the baby was in theatre for preparation. Malaika having become the fierce bold mother after all the anguish and pain in hospital was very furious. She shouted back at the theatre attendant, " how careless are your doctors, how could he not show up knowing he was having a procedure for dialysis today on a baby".

You see baby' situation had gotten worse and he now has developed a kidney infection. The attendant apologized and promised to book a baby for theatre early the following morning.

The next day tests had to be done before the baby was taken into the operating theatre. As Malaika waited anxiously for the results and baby to be taken, she sat besides the window overlooking the parking lot.

Minutes after the attending Neonatal doctor who had worked with them for all these weeks came by stood at the door and said, " Mama! Umekua unaombea mtoto wako?" (Mother have you been praying for your child?)
Malaika immediately shook from her daze looking outside the window turned to the doctor and replied, " ndio!" (Yes)

"Basi Mungu amekuskia!" said the doctor with so much positivity and relief to her voice. (Then God has heard your prayer)

Now to say the least, Malaika who had never cried or broken down in all these weeks of anguish just broke down and fell on her knees in that same corner she had been sitting and wailed. Mixed emotions running through her. She praised God, she prayed with thanks and made an oath to serve God and teach the baby how to serve God for the rest of her days. On her knees crying, that's where Zuberi who had come in early morning found her. She explained it all. They both realized while they were busy complaining about the surgeon' absence the night before, God had actually been renewing and healing baby organs that same night. That's how the baby had his first encounter with God. A miracle. Meanwhile in the next ward a baby with the same condition was in critical condition and his parents needed the dialysis materials from the pharmacy but were not yet able to acquire them. Zuberi immediately handed over what baby was to use that morning.

One family received a miracle of healing for another family to receive a miracle of provision where there was none.

Back home after the discharge, whenever the baby overslept, Malaika would get worried and bend to listen to his heartbeats. She would check and literally count how many times he had urinated (like they did in the hospital) and how many times he was fed. Even, how often he cried.

What the nurse had told her the first time they had gone to the clinic "mama umekua unaweka wapi mtoto" (mother where have you been keeping the baby) kept replaying in her head like a radio cassette. Those words haunted her. Making her feel like it was her fault the baby had gone through this ordeal. She felt so guilty.

She went to the internet to read everything she could find about baby post delivery, about babies who have had jaundice at birth . She just wanted to be perfect.

She was so consumed by the baby during the nights, one eye opened and half her body asleep, during the day washing the baby's clothes and feeding him. She was doing all the baby stuff. Unfortunately Zuberi started feeling like a third wheel in this family triangle.

He started sulking and even told her that she no longer cared about him.

Mama Zuberi noticed her son's moods and started prompting Malaika to do things for Zuberi.

Malaika tried but everytime the baby cried or even coughed, Malaika would naturally switch off.

Malaika thought she too was burning out.

She asked Zuberi to get a domestic worker for her and he didn't approve.

Instead mother tried to chip in with Malaika's chores but Malaika already felt like mother was handling a lot in the household and she would kindly refuse mother's help.

That didn't go down well with the young couple. Malaika looked at it like Zuberi didn't care. Meanwhile Zuberi didn't understand what truly Malaika was going through. In actual sense they never communicated with each other.

It was all talk about the baby and never about their struggle as a couple.

Zuberi got so stressed he moved out of the room.

Malaika felt so guilty about it. Sadly they were past the point of no return.

To a point where Malaika had to summon elder siblings to intervene. They tried to sit the two of them down and talk, but it was like each of them had been holding out a volcano ready to erupt.

Malaika was holding a ton of hurt from way back before the baby was born, and Zuberi had not even revealed the truth because he was in too much pain. Instead he tried as hard also to express his aggravation in the matter.

They tried to patch things up.

However, Malaika by then, too stressed to watch Zuberi who was even more stressed trying to make ends meet. She thought if she didn't move out she would die of depression. In addition, she had lost so much weight. Despite Zuberi' mother feeding them very lavishly, Malaika would never get to digest anything (depression slowly swallowing whatever she ate) even as the baby continued to breastfeed.

One day Malaika just woke up and decided she was going to go back home; the prodigal daughter. She reached out to her mother, swallowing all her pride for the baby's sake.

Brushing aside the fact that her mother had never looked her up in all these months. Her mother received the apology and told her to come back home.

Malaika requested her loving cousin to come pick her up since the journey was long.

That day as they left. Malaika told Zuberi, "Sort yourself out, when you are ready for us we will come back" that is how she left him with a hope that he would organize himself and she would return to him in the near future.

When they got home. Malaika went to live with her older cousin, Mirembe. Cousin Mirembe was great with children and taught Malaika plenty about child care. Meanwhile mother used to send them food and money for baby's milk. You see Malaika had gotten post natal depression which tampered with her hormones and made her milk supply inadequate thus introducing baby to cow milk before six months .

Unfortunately for Malaika her mother used to send this financial support with a lot of backlash and verbal abuse. This disturbed Malaika and she thought it better to get back to employment. This would help her be financially able to support her and her child. It would also get her away from dependency from her mother.

So she started a job hunt. Malaika would leave the baby behind with her cousin and travel to follow up on possibilities here and there through mother's friends and also through Malaika's leads.

Some positions were deep in the rural area, which was a disadvantage to someone with a baby because of very limited amenities. Malaika would have jumped on such offers to adventure in the rural areas, but now things had changed, the baby's needs had to come first.

As weeks passed. she continued communicating with Zuberi on the phone.

Absence makes the heart grow fonder...
Zuberi missed his young family that at one point he travelled all the way to the village where Malaika was staying with her cousin to deliver a big duffle bag with very nice toys and accessories for the baby.

Malaika didn't want to show him the exact house where they stayed so she met him at the trading centre in a public place.

Malaika had promised herself he would have to show some seriousness before she showed him any sign of going back to him. He travelled back almost in the next hour.

As time went on her mother's insults grew worse. On the other hand Zuberi seemed to be making some progress.

The more Malaika looked at the baby, the more she realized she wanted the baby to grow up with his father. She decided since Zuberi was now making an effort in communication, she was ready to patch things up too with him.

It was a time for her to look at which pain she would manage. She chose Zuberi over being home jobless depending on her mother while receiving insults, verbal abuse and degradation from her.

After four months apart, once Zuberi had told her he got a new job in a new city, Malaika made the hardest decision of her life; to move back and make her family matters work for the baby's sake. Every child deserves a stable home.

So once again she asked her cousin who had picked her up four months ago from mama Zuberi' home to help her head back.

Malaika agreed to finance the trip for her cousin and her.

She sent Zuberi a message that she was on the bus headed to his new place. He had moved many districts away, so the journey was very long.

What helped is the money Malaika had saved up for a rainy day when Zuberi had started showing signs of not chipping before the baby was born while Malaika still worked. Matty had advised her to open an account where she

would throw in some small change in case she
was totally stuck.

On reaching the town Zuberi received them so
joyfully.

Took them back to his home.

When they reached Zuberi' place, Malaika
could not believe what she saw. It was a room
in a rental lodge. A bar at the reception.

More of a place where people came in for a
night or two and headed out. Not very homely.
Not a place to raise a baby.

Not a place accommodative for a family.

Malaika excitement died that night but since it
was late and they were tired. Malaika and her
cousin had to think of their dinner that night.
Being a bachelor space with no kitchen ware,
Malaika immediately went into mommy
mode.

They walked to the nearest shopping place and
bought from kitchen ware to baby stuff and
food.

That night they slept very late trying to put things together for dinner and bathroom care before bedtime.

Malaika went to bed once again hurt. Realising Zuberi had not been ready as yet. However she decided there was no going back she had to make it work.

The next day her cousin, feeling the tension in their space, decided to travel back.

That morning Zuberi went to work a few minutes away from where they stayed.

After returning from the bus terminal on escorting her cousin, Malaika, decided it was upto her to make a change by getting a job.

Meanwhile back home mama Malaika was very bitter to discover her daughter had run away from home and this time she disowned her totally, she said she didn't want to see her ever again and Malaika should not appear back again.

Being caught between a rock and a hard place, Malaika knew this was her bed, she had made and had to lie in it no matter how hot it was.

Every morning Zuberi would leave for work, Malaika would also follow without his knowledge but headed in a different direction with CV and application letter. She moved from place to place hoping to get a vacant position. She had mentored many apprentices in her trade for some years and had a great reputation.

Everywhere Malaika went, the baby was on her chest in a baby carrier. The pair looked odd. Malaika had lost so much weight and was like a walking skeleton. So much had weighed her down in this matter emotionally that it affected her physically. People used to wonder if Malaika was a nanny to the baby since she looked frail. Everywhere she went to drop her CV, the baby always had the person behind the desk smiling. Actually the baby was her lucky charm with a positive aura, he always had Malaika and even strangers smiling.

On travelling back to be with Zuberi, Malaika had carried just three pairs of clothes to avoid luggage, since the baby had a lot of things, she had also imagined she would ask Zuberi to buy her more clothes. But as she started job hunting she would wash and recycle these three pieces of clothes. In truth she realized she didn't know how to ask Zuberi to buy her clothes. She would only ask for baby' basic needs. Formula, pampers.

After many days of walking from office to office with no avail, Malaika got to call her former colleague.

He gave her a tip about a vacant placement. When she got there the employer looked at the baby seated on Malaika' laps and told her to start the following week. Just like that she got a job.

***

Malaika had the task to tell Zuberi that she had been going behind his back to look for a job. It was not easy to confront him; he was not happy that she had been going about with the baby. She let him know that she was to commence her new job immediately.

Although she didn't know how she would commute out of town and she worried that the baby was still nursing in between meals. So Malaika asked Zuberi if they could relocate to get a house nearer to her new workplace. Zuberi didn't like the suggestion. He refused.

As days drew nearer without him changing his mind, she told him to help her get a small house near the workplace, which was in the outskirts of town.

Zuberi got angry and it only brought about cold tension in the relationship between the two new parents.

Eventually, he got a place and they moved in. Malaika also needed a babysitter when she went to work. Zuberi got a young lady from his workmates village home. It was a relief.

On the first day as the new sitter started and Zuberi left for the city, Malaika woke up earlier to do all the work and prepared some food for the sitter and baby. Malaika left instructions for the sitter to only take care of the baby. Malaika had never left the baby for so long with a stranger. So she didn't want the sitter to be distracted by house chores, so she asked her to not do anything but play with and keep baby company.
Malaika went to work leaving behind her phone number in case the sitter needed to call.

Work being several blocks away Malaika had to walk to work. She had also planned to be walking back during her break hours to nurse the baby.

Once at work and getting an orientation Malaika's day took off as usual. Until she started feeling funny, like something was happening.

Her heart started pounding, in the pit of her belly it felt like something bad was happening, she got worried and immediately called the sitter but the sitter didn't pick up her call. When she called again the phone was switched off.

Malaika whispered to a colleague that she wanted to slip out of the office briefly because the new sitter had switched off her phone.

Malaika rushed home and on reaching, the house door was wide open.

Malaika's feet went numb, she started shaking, her heart pounding, she was afraid to enter the house because the first thing that came to her was that the baby had been kidnapped by the sitter.

From the spot she was standing you could see through the whole house all doors open. It was as silent as a tomb. Malaika's tears just started trickling, as she reached for her phone which she had placed inside the bra and called Zuberi.

"Zuberi I came back home and the door is wide open and the house is empty," Malaika said in between a teary phone conversation.

She was shaking like a leaf, her feet still planted at the entrance of the door. It was then she noticed the charcoal stove she had left still boiling food for the baby and the sitter still burning.

Meanwhile Zuberi, still talking to her on the phone, also terrified, asked her to get in the house and look at the back room where the balcony was.

That's when her feet moved forward. She walked slowly inside, half listening to instructions from Zuberi.

Baby's toys were all over the floor, she opened the toilet and bathroom as she went by headed to the last room at the back which was the bedroom.

When she reached the bedroom, the phone fell from her hands.

Baby lay on top of the bed, not moving. A silent panic cry escaped Malaika's lips; she was even scared to touch the baby. He had his back to the wall. Malaika went to the floor, picked the phone and spoke into it.

"Zuberi, the baby is here in his baby cot, he's not moving, he's facing the wall, I'm so scared." Malaika was now crying as she spoke.

Zuberi told her to be strong and check if he had any injury on his body.

Malaika did as he told her.

When Malaika turned the baby towards her face he had dried tears and mucus stains in his face but he was asleep.

Malaika removed his clothes slowly and checked him all over for any marks or cuts on his body as Zuberi instructed her on the phone. Baby was unharmed.

Baby opened his eyes from the movement and the feel of her touch.

He started crying anew when he opened his eyes to see his mother.

Malaika lifted him up from his cot and he clung to her shoulder and she hugged him so tightly in her chest. She soothed him till he stopped crying.

Malaika told Zuberi, who had all this time been on the phone, that the baby was okay physically but he was distressed.

Zuberi was on his way back home.

The morning of the ordeal, as Malaika had left for work she summoned the nanny (who looked aloof) for the day's instructions but Malaika had thought it was just first day jitters at a new job for her and so she didn't take it so personally. Malaika had prayed with her just before she walked out with instructions for the day of how to handle the baby. She had promised the nanny that she would be back to nurse the baby and incase of anything she was to call her. Malaika had even loaded the nanny's phone with airtime to call her incase of any emergency.

The baby was generally a jolly child so long as he had a full tummy, dry pamper and someone to play with him. So Malaika was more worried about the nanny than the baby when she left for work that day.

For her to find the nanny had escaped had been a shock.

Malaika went to the shop downstairs to ask the shopkeeper who was also a neighbor if she had seen the nanny. The shopkeeper said she had seen the nanny passby the balcony door and out but didn't really understand what was happening.

When Malaika narrated to her what had happened. The shopkeeper was in shock.

Zuberi came home soon after, he checked the baby all through again just in case the baby needed to be checked by a doctor.

That day Malaika learnt the importance of praying for a baby. She knew that the morning prayer had saved her baby from the evil hands of a bad nanny. From that day forth she never stopped praying over her baby's life. That night after Zuberi reported the nanny to his workmate who had brought her to get work. That night they sat down and praised God for the miracle yet again over the baby's life. Malaika had called work and explained to her new boss of the incident and requested that he give her some days off work to find a sitter, fortunately he was understanding and gave Malaika some days off to sort herself.

Malaika had met a friendly lady who owned a shop halfway between home and Malaika's workplace. She was newly married and Malaika had actually met her on the day she had gone to drop her CV. That day Malaika was thirsty so she went to that shop to have a cold drink. As the lady took to serving Malaika, she really liked the baby and had said she would be praying for Malaika to get that job she had come for. The next time Malaika passed by to tell how she had got the job and was staying not far from her shop.

They quickly became friends. So on the few days as Malaika was home trying to look around for another sitter she had called her new friend. Explained her dilemma.

Her friend had told her she didn't mind the baby staying at the shop through the day as Malaika went to work. They agreed for Malaika not to lose the job, she would leave the baby in the morning and check in the midmorning to nurse him. Malaika dropped the baby every morning as she went to work, leaving at the shop all baby's requirements during the day.

Her friend enjoyed having a baby and told Malaika it was good practice for her as she and her husband were hoping and praying to conceive one day.

This was a great solution for Zuberi and Malaika. The baby also enjoyed his time out since there was a lot of activity at the shop.

It was not easy for Maliaka after the nanny incident, but she had to trust the God that saved the baby would continue to keep him safe.

Malaika resumed work after a couple of days with the baby always looking forward to going out of the house and going to the shop.

Malaika had originally travelled from her parents home to join Zuberi with only a few pieces of clothes.

Zuberi had not yet thought of buying her clothes and so she switched between these four pieces of clothes for months until she got her first salary.

As time went by Zuberi and Malaika had reduced their relationship to that of roommates other than that of a married couple. The only thing that they shared was that of a little one that both loved very much.

Malaika was scared of Zuberi. She had heard a lot about men that forced their partners to sleep with them. Everytime Zuberi came home, she would think that would be the day. But Zuberi had never touched or physically hurt her.

Eventually Zuberi moved out since they had started having loads of verbal fights and both had thought it was not healthy for the baby to have two unhappy parents.

After weeks apart Zuberi had invited Malaika to go to church with him. She met his friends. He had already got a community of people around him.

Malaika worked at the station for almost a year but they had frequent salary arrears which made her look for another job.

On meeting his community of friends, she attempted a job interview on one of these occasions and got a new job placement.

Zuberi who would come to visit the baby since both parents now lived separately. Zuberi was trying to push for a reconciliation so much so he could be with Malaika.

Unfortunately by that time Malaika was burnt out from the loads of hurt from Zuberi. She decided to focus on raising the baby and being the best mother she could be.

Malaika would call Zuberi for child support and remind him to do his part and this annoyed her.

Zuberi would tell her, she also had a job and so she could do as well as she wanted him to. He would remind that she left him once. Zuberi continually reminded her how her mother had not approved of him. This always hurt Malaika.

Malaika thought it wise to inquire about what the responsibilities of separated parents were, from a mutual friend (a lawyer). When Zuberi learnt about this, he was very mad.

He retaliated by going to child protection services and reported Malaika.

Malaika got served and was to report to this office every end month to receive some money through the office and Zuberi was allowed to pick up the baby during weekends and take him out, it counted as visitation rights. Zuberi had accused Malaika of refusing him access to the baby. The children's court said Malaika was guilty. He would give her a meagre amount stashed in an envelope.

Unfortunately Malaika had only asked the lawyer friend to get advice on how Zuberi could increase child support finances.

At this time he was earning a good amount of money so Malaika had been hurt as to why she had to always quarrel or beg for him to part with money. Meanwhile, Zuberi had interpreted the whole thing so differently. and thought she wanted to block him from his child.

When Malaika was served by the child protection services, she was devastated and broken that Zuberi would think so negatively of her, yet she had sacrificed so much for him and for their love. It pained her too that Zuberi had never actually ever known that Malaika had abandoned her family for him and he continued to hurt her.

Every month as she went to pick the financial envelope from the child protective services, she felt humiliated and broken, like Zuberi had reduced her to a criminal. What made it worse, the offices had never taken time to call her and hear her side of the story. They had assumed Zuberi was the wronged party.

From then on when Zuberi came to pick up the baby, Malaika could not bear to see Zuberi.

She was full of pain, like someone had pierced a spear in the depth of her heart.

Time went by and Malaika realized how the pain was slowly consuming her. She made a decision to take counseling from mutual people who could talk to both Zuberi and her.

Zuberi even went for counseling from his fellow married friends.

These friends looking at both sides objectively tried to patch them together.

It seemed like things started to fall back in place.

Zuberi got to a point where he wanted to work for his family.

Zuberi buried himself in wanting to achieve but things were not working. He changed career and jobs. His mind so focused that he got lost in himself.

Baby started school.

Malaika thought the baby needed the best.

All this time Zuberi never shared anything personal with her.

When Malaika tried to brooch any personal topics he would push her aside.

When money was needed or they talked about money, he would get offended and tell her, she too worked and had money.

When Malaika wanted to bring ideas for them to develop. Zuberi always got annoyed saying since "had a degree" she thought she was better than him.

It was hard just being on the same page.

Malaika even realized it was hard for him to talk about money.

She had arranged to speak to the headteacher after the baby changed from an expensive school and had gone to a cheaper school. Malaika would look for the money and request the headteacher not to tell the father. Malaika didn't want to hurt Zuberi' feelings.

Zuberi was determined to be the best of the best but in the back of it all losing his family and in as much as Zuberi and Malaika tried they kept slipping from each other.

Baby being the only factor bringing them together.

Malaika was fighting so hard to hold onto the man she loved and in trying so hard, she was making many mistakes in the heat of those moments and speaking hurtful words to him and him doubling those words with more heated arguments.

Once again they parted ways.

Zuberi relocated to a different city for work. He continued to keep his visits to the baby.

The one thing Malaika knew was that Zuberi had grown to be a loving father. He had learned how to father in his absent moments.

Malaika had told herself she may still struggle to be on the same page with Zuberi but she would never take the baby away from his father. She knew the importance of a father and son bond.

Fathering long distance, Zuberi and the baby would spend lots of time on the phone.

When Zuberi relocated, it was hard. Malaika would call him begging him to send money. Sometimes he would take a while. Things being hard in the new city and him juggling between jobs.

A young child had lots of needs Malaika could not do it alone. When it hit rock bottom, Malaika would call Zuberi demanding for help.

Malaika would tell Zuberi, "I have never asked you for anything but to please provide for the baby without me asking, it's all I'm begging of you."

She used to get frustrated at such times.

Once Zuberi travelled. Malaika had told him to wait till morning to come by to see the baby.

Zuberi had insisted and came at night.

Malaika had been so annoyed. She refused to let him in the house that night. She told Zuberi that the baby would not understand why his father was coming in for a few minutes and heading out while he had been away for many weeks in another town working.

Malaika had told Zuberi the baby would be confused why his father was not spending a night at home. Zuberi thought Malaika was denying him access and got very annoyed. He had nowhere to go since it was late.

Malaika told him to go spend his night at his friend's place.

Zuberi instead went to a mutual friend and said Malaika had refused him to see his son.

The truth is that Malaika and Zuberi' relationship had spiralled to a toxic kind.

They loved each other but because they barely communicated, it just tore them away from each other.

Zuberi was good to everyone, a kind soul but when it came to his association with Malaika it just didn't add up as both wished.

****

It seems to me that my life has been a series of cycles, each one seeming to bring me closer to some reality that is still unclear to me.

In my 20s I was a square peg trying to fit into a round hole. Who I was was a mystery to me; but if it did exist, she was buried in my secrets.

My 30's were years of flexing my creative muscles and exploring my possibilities, and I found teaching, and fell in love with my students; every year, without fail, I would fall in love with them, and celebrate their graduation as I sent them off into the world, and then turned and started to fall in love with the next year's students. It was when I turned 30 that I finally felt people could stop saying I was too young to know what I was talking about. In my 30's I explored the occult and started reading tarot cards, and following astrology through my sister, Mary.

But who I was was buried under fear and denial, and was easily distracted by the reality of my sister battling cancer for a year before her death. I created a very convincing mask with which to face the world. My idealism was in full force, and my delusion was concrete and reinforced by responsibilities, and an attempt to meet them.

My 40's brought me to my knees, emotionally, psychologically, and spiritually. In that decade I learned how flawed I am. But despite those flaws, I am a survivor.

Forty is also the age when we start taking medication... No one over 40 is medication free.... But then again, a century ago people didn't live as long as we do.

I had this idealized version of what life was supposed to be; a Utopian fantasy that was a conglomeration of visions where Camelot was not too far-fetched.

They say that a cynic is an idealist who has had too much of a dose of reality. But cynicism was very uncomfortable for me.

***

The baby now four years old had a baby-sitter, very motherly.

This sitter used to come early in the morning, and found Malaika had prepared the baby ready for school. The babysitter took him to school then picked him up later in the afternoon.

Meanwhile Malaika would rush to work.

Finally, after months of routine and order :

Malaika received a call requesting for a mobile money transfer, in the middle of the night from a stranger saying that the sitter had attempted to kill herself while she was with her own children and husband. She had self inflicted cuts all over her body. Money was needed that night at the local hospital to nurse the babysitter.

By that time Malaika lived on a minimum wage and had no money to spare after paying her baby sitter salary a few days ago .

The following day as she rushed to take the baby to school before heading to work, she was told by a few neighbors that it was not the first time that the sitter had tried to harm herself.

Malaika was shocked at this revelation. she wondered how the neighbors could have let her go on to use the services of the sitter knowing that she needed medical help.

The new morning routine consisted of Malaika walking the baby to the neighbor who had agreed to drop and pick up the baby. The neighbor had a child at the same school as the baby.

The children would play together at the neighbor' house till Malaika came to collect the baby in the evening as she returned from work.

During her mini-night shifts when her apprentices needed her, Malaika would bring along baby to work.

As the school year ended, Zuberi and Mama Zuberi suggested it was better for the baby to travel to stay with them since Malaika had searched in vain to find a baby sitter.

That's how the baby ended up living with his grandma and his father.

It had started as a brief solution to a problem (no babysitter). Then grandma thought it would be wise if the baby stayed and registered for a new school near her home.

Even before the baby relocated to stay with his grandma, Zuberi had always travelled with the baby during brief breaks to spend time with his child so the baby would get to learn his paternal side.

The only difference was that this time it seemed like a long departure. Malaika had never been away from baby for many days.

She would break down in tears, missing the baby, missing Zuberi, the love of her life. It's like everything had been taken leaving her empty.

She felt like she had fought so hard just to have these two by her side and she had failed miserably.

Malaika always spoke to the baby on the phone everyday. But it was hard, especially when the baby would ask her why she was not coming.

He would cry over the phone for his mum. Baby was in good hands with his grandma who loved him with all her being. On the day he started school his grandma would carry him on her back to take him to school barely a few blocks from her home.

His dad on the other hand now became an amazing dad picking from where Malaika had left with parenting baby.

Malaika realized she had carried so much pain in her heart from the seperation, she needed a fresh start, a clean mind.

So the next job offer that came by, meant Malaika had to travel far away with hope that once settled for a few months. She would go bring the baby to join her. Unfortunately on reaching everything was not as she expected. The benefits and allowance could not enable her to bring the baby.

Communication continued between the small family through telephone.
Giving her a different perspective to life. She now appreciated Zuberi' efforts in the past although he had never taken time to share with her all his struggles. Somehow emotionally, mentally and physically her pains faded one by one.

She kept hoping that Zuberi would pursue her again. Unfortunately it never came.

She still lit a candle for him. He never noticed any of that probably also dealing with his own issues and coming to terms with life.

Zuberi buried himself into fatherhood.

It became harder as years went by for the baby to join Malaika in the far away land since there were no favorable conditions at her work place.

After two years Malaika was pleased that the baby had his father to grow up with. She had always wanted the baby to have his father close. Regardless that their relationship as parents had not worked.

Malaika always picked up the baby and stayed at her friend's house till the school break would end then return the baby to his grandma's house where the baby's father stayed.

As years went by, the baby started getting curious and asking questions as to why his dad and mum were not together like other children' parents.

The more years went by Zuberi never said anything. At times she would telephone him and he would ignore, "Malaika what do you want from me?" he would say.

Zuberi had never recovered from the first day when Malaika walked away from him, when she had told him, "When you are ready for us, I will come back."

Years down the road, Zuberi moved on, he met a wonderful lady.

Malaika was truly happy for him.

She was happy for her friend, the father of her child.

Malaika discovered this during her holiday time with the baby. As they had dinner, mother and child, baby blurted out, "Mum, do you know I have a new mother?"

Malaika felt like her world axis had been shifted, like a place deep inside Zuberi' soul had been replaced.

But she never expressed her pain to the baby. She instead told him, "That is a blessing my baby, it means you have two mamas who will love you so much. You are blessed to have so much love around you." She went on to reassure the baby, " Yes, if your daddy is happy, it is a good thing to be happy for him and with him."

That is how the baby took to liking his new mum.

Malaika felt empty. She felt sad she had lost the love of her life. Someone she had fought so hard to be with and lost. However she told herself if he was happy that was all that mattered. She chose to be happy for him. Almost nine years of holding a candle and now blown by the wind.

For the rest of her life she chose to remember the happy moments. Also to appreciate how far life had pushed them to be better individuals, better parents and also how they had grown as individuals.

She hoped that she too would eventually find someone she would open her heart too and love again.

Always the positive one despite all life had thrown her way. She chose to hope. Dream again. Manifest a great future for her and her child.

She buried herself in long distance motherhood, work, doing things she had always dreamt to do and set new aspirations to life. She chose to go through a journey of self discovery and healing from all her past wounds. A new dawn.

***

All the pending deaths occurred by the time I hit 50. I was truly alone. No one else required me to wear a mask. I have to say I peaked in my 50's. It was my best decade. I felt successful, I felt like I had finally come into my own. I was at the top of the pyramid of needs. AND then I fell in love. Head over heels, like a fool on drugs...

I'd lost 85 pounds and finally "saw" myself... not the mask I'd been wearing, but the mask behind the mask. The mask behind all of the other masks; my face unmasked.

And then I turned 60..... And I started to hemorrhage... I was weeping every day... my career had been taken from me by a fool, and I was consumed by rage that could not be expressed. I was diagnosed with cancer. My 60's were filled by cancer, and my mortality. And I married my "Evil"; "Every rose has its thorn" (Brett Michaels). I survived because he loved me. And I survive still because of him.

But my 60's brought poverty to my life. My economic world collapsed and I was worried all the time. Once Joe's business collapsed around him I learned how to beg, and I learned how to ask for help, and humbled myself. Struggled to forgive myself for failing; failing to see "illness" as a possibility on this journey, and so never planned for the possibility.

I desperately tried to hold onto my "Middle Class" status; afterall, I was a professional; I was educated, talented... but I felt defeated and lost most of the time. My 60's brought self realization, that I am only now trying to find some hindsight from which to view it.

My 70's have been a revelation of answered prayers that started when I was tired of feeling like shit every day; and thinking about only depressing crap every day... And thinking I could do anything about anything.... What a waste of time and energy,,,

At 70 I decided to accept the things I can not change.

So now I am off the hook. And nothing is my problem.... It'll work out somehow...

.... And this is just a prelude ...

ABOUT THE AUTHORS

Hellen Nakhone Madadi

A Teacher, Motivational Speaker, Podcaster on Anchor FM Priceless Moments with Hellen Madadi, Content Creator/ Poet (helensera) and Mother. Very passionate about child issues and Intentional Parenting.

Collaborating with Rose Terranova Cirigliano in this amazing book KINDRED- In her eyes/ In her mind, has been an amazing journey of discovery and growth. Bringing out the best of 2020/ 2021.

Rose Terranova Cirigliano-

I am a retired teacher; 17 years in the classroom, (Junior High), and then 8 years on TV. I wrote, hosted, and produced educational programs for the Catholic Diocese of Brooklyn and Queens. On the side I was the director of a parish theater group mounting two productions each year, one a musical play, and the other a Cabaret. I am a classically trained singer, and did recitals from 1983 through 2000. I met Lewis Crystal in 1979 when I worked at HBJ Bookstore with him and Brigitte. I've always written poetry, from when I was in my teens. Lewis enabled me to make some of my private writing public. And I have been grateful ever since. I currently edit a seasonal anthology for FM Magazine, and other works from an international group of authors through a small publishing company, ROSE BOOKS, an affiliate of AVENUE U PUBLISHERS, [Lewis Crystal (owner)].